D0329571

MORMON GROWN GAY

Brandea J. Kelley, PA-C

BALBOA.
PRESS
A DIVISION OF HAY HOUSE

Copyright © 2016 Brandea J. Kelley.

All rights reserved. No part of this book may be used or reproduced by any means, graphic, electronic, or mechanical, including photocopying, recording, taping or by any information storage retrieval system without the written permission of the author except in the case of brief quotations embodied in critical articles and reviews.

Balboa Press books may be ordered through booksellers or by contacting:

Balboa Press
A Division of Hay House
1663 Liberty Drive
Bloomington, IN 47403
www.balboapress.com
1 (877) 407-4847

Because of the dynamic nature of the Internet, any web addresses or links contained in this book may have changed since publication and may no longer be valid. The views expressed in this work are solely those of the author and do not necessarily reflect the views of the publisher, and the publisher hereby disclaims any responsibility for them.

The author of this book does not dispense medical advice or prescribe the use of any technique as a form of treatment for physical, emotional, or medical problems without the advice of a physician, either directly or indirectly. The intent of the author is only to offer information of a general nature to help you in your quest for emotional and spiritual well-being. In the event you use any of the information in this book for yourself, which is your constitutional right, the author and the publisher assume no responsibility for your actions.

Any people depicted in stock imagery provided by Thinkstock are models, and such images are being used for illustrative purposes only.
Certain stock imagery © Thinkstock.

Print information available on the last page.

ISBN: 978-1-5043-6895-7 (sc)
ISBN: 978-1-5043-6896-4 (e)

Balboa Press rev. date: 01/06/2017

PREFACE

What on earth do I have to say that's worthy of asking busy people to take time out of their lives to read?

This is what I am asking myself as I plunk along on my computer in my little backyard studio, temporarily undaunted by the fact that I'm not a "real" writer. I don't expertly craft sentences and words like the authors I have loved over the years, punctuating gracefully and lilting with delicate descriptives. I wasn't trained for this. I cringe at the abuse of the comma in my run-on roller-coasters. Having adopted texting as my primary form of communication, I have devolved to scrawling abbreviated toddler-worthy words, while lazily relying on an emoticon to portray context and feeling instead of the pesky semblance of noun, pronoun, adjective, and verb- and whatever else there is, I don't really remember. I have a shiny, used thesaurus, like any 6th grader.

So.... These are my writing credentials, but buckle up, here we go. It's nice to meet you.

I may have contracted the "I can do this" grandiose bug by reading Ray Bradbury's words in *Zen in the Art of Writing*, which I picked up after the nagging urge to write this book wouldn't leave. I thought his amazing talent would put me in my place, and then I could get on with other things I know I can do in life.

However, reading his heated words did the opposite:

> What do you think of the world? You, the prism, measure the light of the world; it burns through your mind to throw a different spectroscopic reading onto

white paper than anyone else anywhere can throw. Let the world burn through you. Throw the prism light, white hot, on paper. Make your own individual spectroscopic reading. Then, you, a new element, are discovered, charted, named! ... There is only one type of story in the world. Your story.

(By the way, see how many commas are in that last sentence?)

Instead of dissuading me, Bradbury's words inspired me. Plus, I realized I'm not writing for the masses or to impress anyone. I'm only writing my little story to help a few people and hopefully encourage those around them in the small corner of the world where I came from, then ran from. (This is possibly only ten people, if my family members agree to a courtesy read). So it really takes the pressure off. But in all honesty, if this helps even one LGBT reader or loved one who is trying to help and understand them, then I'm glad to try my hand at this daunting business of book writing.

Since my childhood, I have come alive through the words of amazing writers, having been a voracious reader since the third grade. Those beautiful storytellers transformed my young world. I loved the opportunity each book provided to adventurously travel to unfamiliar distant lands, and to understand and experience things a sheltered Mormon girl, born and bred in Salt Lake City, just didn't come across in her real life. Which was a heck-of-a lot of things. I used to hide under my blanket with a flashlight, reading anything from the science fiction greats that I could get my grubby hands on. I adventured with Frank Herbert, J.R.R Tolkien, and Anne Rice, and adored the wordsmiths Ray Bradbury, Maya Angelou, and Barbara Kingsolver. Any one of these I could get my hands on would accompany me through the night and into the wee hours of the morning. Yes, I was the geek who faked sick for school because I couldn't part with Lewis Carroll until sunrise.

I wouldn't smudge the art by suggesting that I am anything more than an amateur with a pen and a purpose. Having to revisit the proper use of punctuation- a special form of torture in middle school- is no less painful in the misty, forgetful sunset of my forties. Painful, and very bossy, punctuation is. Much like my 6-year-old: "Aren't you supposed to slow down for yellow lights and *not* go faster?" You're driving wrong, you know. You're being dangerous."

I love that.

So if you would, please excuse my imperfect presentation, enjoy our Mormon brand swear words, and accompany the revisitation of my journey.

CHAPTER 1

NO WAY; I'M A GAY

I write this to tell a story that me and those close to me needed to read when I was a young, and it was nowhere to be found.

Surprise! You're a gay.

You've finally figured it out. You can't change it, and a conventional, predictable life is out of the question for you now. Also, according to your religion, you won't be achieving Godhood and progressing to the Celestial Kingdom after your death, which has been your utmost aspiration all of your holy Mormon life, soooooo. That's the launchpad for this shizzleshow.

As you might imagine, this is a scorching hot mess at first. The part that is not well publicized, at least not in any of the Mormon-sponsored or associated literature I could find, is that there is really nothing wrong with you.

This will get better.

Things look up quickly as you come to understand that what you were taught about homosexuality was fear based, human judgment, and God doesn't play by limited human rule books. People who live lives alternative to the heterosexual majority help to expand humanity's vision of what love really is, and potentially have the power to persuade people to think with a higher mind. To branch out and love creatively, openly, and unconditionally, the way love is meant to be! Understand that being gay, bisexual, transgendered or anything "outside the norm" is an identifying *gift* from your Source or God or Universal Power (however you want to refer to it). There are throngs of people like us; outsiders, living spiritually fulfilled and happy lives. Examples like Jordan Bach abound (I invite you to explore his inspiring website at www.thebachbook.com). We are not intended to live lovelessly, and just resist the temptation to love and be loved because someone told you it would prove your devotion to God. We survive and surmount the darkness of our human predicament by loving another, and learning to be loved. The one that made you would not rob you of that.

You can escape from the people who treat you poorly, or they will change with you. You can have an amazing life worth looking forward to, and you will have real love if that's what you want. You are not damned to hell, or a sinner taking a ride there in a hand-basket. We are all different in the way that we were made, and no one can speculate on the way God would *judge* the people he made, that is, if you must believe in a judging icky thunder-bolt tossin' God. The problem at it's root is only humans judging other humans. The Mormon (or any other formal religious) way is not the *only* way to God, no matter how spiritually connected you feel to your religion now. You may have felt the spirit, that buzzing of your higher power upon you in a church, and by association, feel that leaving that would be insanity. But religion doesn't have the market on God's love and spiritual connection- they enjoy it just like everyone else, and so many of the religious cultivate it beautifully. But as you leave that church, which they may require, don't fear that you are leaving the only portal to a higher power. Your Source- the One who made you- made you different on purpose, and will always be there for you. "God don't make no mistakes!". No *one* way can be the only right way. The road to God has many trails, and one who insists that their religion is right and all others are wrong truly can't be trusted. This stoic intolerance is reminiscent of playgroud bickering, birthing the types that "fight" for God, the greatest moronic oxymoron of all time. Just try looking at this life from a new perspective for a while, without letting the indoctrinated judgment voice you know slip in to your head until the dust settles and you know in your own heart that it's true. Please don't give a moment's consideration to ending your precious life in shame before you get the chance to find these truths for yourself.

When you realize you are gay, your life and your spirituality may feel like it falls apart. Your understanding of your Source will evolve over time. God can become a kindred spirit, a co-captain and guide, instead of a punitive deity making behavioral check-boxes in the sky. No, it's not rationalizing (I can hear your trained Mormon brain challenging). It's spiritually expanding. Your understanding of the powers that be will eventually become clearer. For you, God may metamorphasize, expand, or take a hike to leave you with an entirely new perception. Spirituality and religion are not synonymous. I didn't lose that feeling of a higher power in my life when I left the church, except when I intentionally ignored my higher power when I was pouting about my lot in life like a toothless 5 year old who's sand shovel was stolen by the sea. If anything I became *more* integrated with a higher power, having to rely so heavily on emotional support from above and inside myself rather than the support of those around me. The understanding that others have of you will change too! This is evidenced by the Supreme Court ruling to uphold gay marriage across the United States in 2015, followed by my staunchly religious father's complete change of heart on LGBT issues, though his beloved church's stance has gone the opposite way.

The American people came to our aid in assisting the achievement of a basic human right to marry, whether they agree with our "lifestyle" or not. I offer my thanks to our "hetero" allies who get what we've gone through, and show love even though it's not their issue. That really is selfless and gracious; I have so many people like this to thank in my life. The court's decision was a landmark time I never thought my eyes would see. I'm touched to tears when I think about the outpouring of love this decision represented. On June 26, 2015 the White House wore rainbow colors.

We're no longer struggling alone.

With the Supreme Court's ruling, I legally married my wife,

and my family enjoys the benefits of marriage today. There is much to celebrate, but there is more yet to do. To rest on the laurels of 2015 without working hard to continue inclusion without prejudice would be lazy and lame. It's not who my proud Canadian mom raised me to be. Living as I do now, a happy and fulfilled, largely cozy and unthreatened life in Seattle, I forget that many like me still live lives filled with fear for loving who they do. This could be you or someone you know. I take for granted the open-minded, effortless interspersal of gays into our communities. We live in our communities without much reference to the fact that our genders are matching. It's just another detail that blends into the background over time when you know people. Being gay is *less* interesting than this week's story of my son pulling poop marbles out of his diaper and hiding them around the house like the excremental Easter Bunny. But it's still *more* entertaining than a Kardashian outing posted next to a picture of her oiling her haunches on a magazine cover. (That's just my opinion; I could be wrong).

Being gay just doesn't feel like that big of a deal any more, though it nearly ended my life as a hopeless and ashamed 18-year-old.

I recently rekindled a loving relationship with my extremely religious father after spending most of my adult years estranged from him for my being gay. I then happened upon my old journal, which was an overture to coming out of the closet as a member of the Mormon Church in Utah and working through my value system to figure it all out. I realized I had become comfortably apathetic, having jumped (-er, lurched) over my hurdles and run happily away from the ever-shrinking threats in my rear view mirror. I had bopped around, basking in my now happy life, with my happy wife, in my happy gay town with my skippy pants on, not caring enough about the continuing plight of other people like us elsewhere. So I thought hard about ways I could help.

Donating money to LGBT funds and scholarships.

Being out of the closet at work, even when it's uncomfortable.

Having a Human Rights Campaign sticker on my car?

Supporting artists and establishments with supportive policies?

It didn't feel like enough. My heart broke every time I heard of another gay Mormon suicide (see the afterword for true and depressing data), and I wanted to do more.

So I wrote this story. Telling it is *that* thing—my contribution to the cause that will hopefully help someone. I want to give LGBT people who may read this some hope, a laugh, or just a happy gay ending to look at after going through a lot to feel good about who they are. Perhaps I can help those who are struggling to understand gay and transgendered people as well.

I kept painfully detailed records of the "coming out" process I went through, because it helped me cope with what I was going through without having to tell anyone. As a Mormon, "coming out" was essentially embracing the hell I was "choosing" by leaving the heavenly, encapsulating cocoon of the Mormon Church, as it were. Why would I *choose* this? Because fitting in, making my family proud, having friends, and a pretty clear life plan was just not doin' it for me. I just wanted to—*ya know*—shake it up. Like a shaken-baby-kind-of horror shake. Who isn't looking for that real life horror show, really? Yeah.

My parents have been kind enough to relay their experiences and the way they have come to think of the issue, and both are loving and accepting toward me, while remaining upstanding members of the LDS church. I hope their generous contributions to this can help someone as well.

This is the gist of my journey, regurgitated and lawlessly rearranged from the journal I kept during that time. It's paraphrased, because wow, I was peeved (quite colorful language for a lil' Mormon girl, and boatloads of heck's fury appropriately and inappropriately directed). Do appreciate my Mormon swears, which I will pepper ever so carefully throughout this text for your reading pleasure, for flashback fun, and for propriety for young ones. From the freaked out, embarrassed, religion-blighted girl I was to the amazingly happy and fulfilled, wife and kid-having, gay lady-mom I am now, I have had a long journey to become the unlikely daughter my parents are proud of. I'm proud of the progress I have made too, and hope I can give back some of the healing wealth that has been given to me by so many.

By the way, I'm strongly against bashing people in a religion who are just trying to do good. So you won't hear me criticize church members, or even bash the governing body in anger. Despite some perhaps unconventional beliefs at the religion's core, I see many Mormons and religious people as just trying to help others and be better people. Some members stay with the church they were raised in out of respect for their families; some have inertia; some just want to do right and belonging to the church helps them in that goal, though they may not know or even agree with some of the more specific dictates within the religion. I don't want to offend my family and so many friends who are good people to their core, who ascribe to the Mormon Church. So, with respect for them, and with hope for better care of LGBT people, here is my story.

Chapter 2

Wuvvv Is What Bwings Us Togevewww ... Today

I never in a million frickin' years expected to get married *legally* to the woman I loved in my lifetime, not to mention having that marriage upheld federally throughout our nation. I remember feeling bad for those who campaigned so hard and wanted it so much, because I thought they were setting themselves up for a huge let-down. I supported the Human Rights Campaign and signed and participated in everything that came my way, but I never instigated anything of substance on my own. I was shocked when gay marriage was legalized, and in the back of my mind I'm still secretly braced for a revocation.

After devaluing the laws of man for so many years due to a shortsighted and disconnected deciding body, I had a renewal of faith in the system with this ruling. Nicole and I were surprised that suddenly in 2013 we could marry lawfully, and we did so for a few reasons. Our first reason was to confirm our relationship out there in the public eye. We were for each other what we had both always wanted; this was clear to us without a piece of paper or a ceremony. We wanted to do it in part to show the world the true numbers of LGBTs who want to marry and our intention as a group to have meaningful, significant relationships over the span of our lives. Secondly, we wanted to have our relationships recognized for personal, financial, and legal reasons. Finally, we did it to thank all those who had worked so tirelessly to make it happen: campaigning, investing time and energy, and inspiring persistence until social justice was served for us. The people in this movement made amazing progress—progress I thought would never be made in my lifetime. They made it for our family, and we have profound gratitude for their work.

It feels so good to be honest and fearless in acknowledging the one I love. So often people still stay closeted to avoid unnecessary judgment or persecution. Or they just want privacy. This was often my preference while still in Utah: No one needs to know who I'm in love with but me. Later I had to admit that fear and shame, more than a private nature, influenced my cover. When love is tainted like that, it pervades everything in your life, though you don't really know it's happening. It's like a hidden leak in your shrinking pond of integrity that you don't know is there until you're flopping in the shallows. Lies of omission still feel like lies. No, one doesn't have to have full disclosure at work or with friends. Lord knows the unwanted mental images we would receive in that case. But I felt, if I fake this, what else would I fake? Would I become a fraud, fudging my way through life, refusing to honestly participate and engage with people as a habit?

I rationalized to myself, "No one wants a stereotypical lesbo in their grill. It's too weird; people don't want to be uncomfortable." I didn't want to be the topic of scandalous discussion." I didn't want people imagining my sex life—it's embarassing. I didn't want the room to get quiet when I walked in. I didn't want to be pigeonholed and stereotyped. I refused to wear Birkenstocks even though I admit I really wanted to.

Mother trucker, my feet hurt!...

As minorities however, with deficient human rights, LGTBQ people need to be visible even when it's uncomfortable. The one whom everyone looks up to and thinks is "normal, just like everyone else" or even a "hero" is the one who often hides the longest. Because they can!

They aren't stereotypically "other than hetero." No male lisp, limp wrist, effeminate tendencies, or alternately in women, no strut, giveaway "boy" hair (as my daughter lovingly calls mine), or butchy demeanor. They look right to gender and are often sizzling hot about it! They're also the ones, when they do come out, who shake biased people's foundation of what "gay" is. They reset them, and they reset "us."

I have nothing against the rainbow-painted flaming peacock queen first on the float for the Pride parade, or the spiky, slightly angry dyke-on-a-bike in black leather, but they are not always the easiest people for the world to warm to, other queers included! This person does not represent all of us, but the extreme stereotypes, or someone acting like a jackwagon at a pride parade is often the first and only one to make it to camera.

So for those in the closet, please expand out already. The upsides are worth the down! We now enjoy a life that has been fought for and won by so many brave individuals over the years, from old-school Harvey Milk to modern day Ben Cohen, Jodi Foster, and Andersen Cooper. In coming out, you recognize and show appreciation for their efforts. This is not the same world that it was. People like Neil Patrick Harris, Matt Bomer (sigh), Ellen DeGeneres and countless others have made this world kinder and safer for you. Most importantly, every person deserves the joy that comes from living honestly and authentically.

What I *didn't* expect from coming out is that something snapped inside me, and loving myself and everyone else became easier. Light flooded through the tainted lenses of my interactions with people whose judgement I feared previously. Now I saw that they were just human. Flawed as frack, but generally well meaning and not to be feared. I was free of this heavy shadow of shame I didn't even realize had been shrouding me for so long. I learned that shame had poisoned me all the way to the cobwebby, dark corners of my life that I didn't know had been cultivated. When that shame was finally gone, it was a breathtaking change in me, and to follow, in the way others reacted to me. When I was no longer mortified for being me, others picked up on the inference that *I had no reason to be.* Yes, there were times it was hard, and I wanted to crawl under a rock and die five times. It's not easy. But each generation has an easier go of it when we are true to who we are, and as people understand us better, it's a chain reaction that improves the state of the world for the next round.

I'd like to paraphrase Ellen Page's beautifully stated words in her coming out speech:

> I'm tired of hiding, and I'm tired of lying by omission. I suffered for years because I was scared to be out. My spirit suffered, my mental health suffered, and my relationship suffered. And I'm standing here today with all of you on the other side of that pain. ... But what I have learned is that love—the beauty of it, the joy of it, and yes, even the pain of it, is the most incredible gift to give and to receive as a human being. We deserve to experience love fully, equally, without shame and without compromise. There are too many kids out there suffering from bullying, rejection, or mistreatment because of who they are. Too many dropouts, too much abuse, too many homeless, too many suicides. You can change that, and you are changing it. Thank you for giving me hope, and thank you for changing the world for people like me.

When I look at my wife and our two kids in our loving household, despite some hot messes I made on my path to arrive here, I now feel like this crazy journey has been a success story. I'm at peace with who I am, and I'm so grateful to those who helped me get here. Don't think I have a fat head; I still need to develop in so many other areas, it's not even funny. The ability to actually get up and exercise when my alarm goes off, realizing my inspired career path (what I really want to be when I grow up), controlling my temper, driving without distraction, cursing like a sailor, saving money, avoiding foods deemed unhealthy though delicious, holding my tongue and speaking my mind at the right times—these are all skills I still work hard (usually) to obtain. I have much to work on, but I've made progress in being comfortable in my own gay skin, and for that I'm deeply grateful.

I wish I had known back then the possibility of the life I have now. I would have had more courage getting through the dark and lonely idea of what life would hold for me after leaving the church and then "living" gay. I wouldn't have felt so hopeless. I wouldn't have been so reckless, and, on more than one night, so dangerously tempting my end, wishing for the pain of this life to be over.

Society as a whole is coming around slowly but surely. But it still isn't good enough when a person is made to feel like death is a better option than living because she loves someone of the same gender. By definition, love can't be God's "testing" tool. Love is the cure for murky badness, and is what we're supposed to figure out while we're on this planet. To treat any form of adult, consensual, and real love as a sin is like calling the cure for a disease its cause.

That a loving God or Source (for lack of a better non-denominational definition) would create us to feel a love toward someone other than the norm, and then punish us for that love is beyond my comprehension. And, you have to admit, there sure are a lot of us. This is no fluke or "oops, my bad" moment in the chemistry lab of human creation. It's not just a hormonal surge in utero, a mistake in upbringing, or a gene flipped upside down in a moment of creational imperfection that occurred thousands and thousands of times. It has not been found to come about by any single cause. We're an extremely common thing! It might make sense to conclude God doesn't make "mistakes" on this scale, just sayin'.

Becoming a parent convinced me further there is no way a spiritual parent would make me gay and then tell me the love I feel is evil—as a challenge to my devotion or otherwise.

The thing I encourage people to focus on instead—is every good thing that can come to be in this world. Sunsets, bacon, art and culture, noodles, new babies, the best burger ever, old growth forests, red wine, sports, puppies, chocolate, scuba diving, and good music for starters. Looking through the swimming pools in the eyes of the one who loves you during your last hours in this world, wondering how you'll go on without him and wanting only them there—that's what love and life is about. It's not the gender of those who are feeling it that matters. Love is spiritual, human progress; it's what makes us different and special beings on this planet. I know, I may be making people hurl with cheesy love-song-overdose (where I usually change the station while making gagging noises), but it has to be here because at the heart of the mistreatment of LGBTs is judgement of *whom one loves*. Love is not about sex. There is nothing as all-encompassing and uplifted as true love between people. Period.

I hope that the people I love who are practicing Mormons will read this. I think good people may feel deep down that at least some of what I'm saying is true, even if envisioning gay sex or having a sex reassignment is downright perplexing or gross to them. It is! Envisioning the sex of MOST of the general population is also completely gross. The tiny population of airbrushed beautiful movie stars aside, do you want people thinking in detail of you or your parents having sex with—whomever? Mental pictures? Perplexing as to how ... why ... ugh, stop. The point is, It's *not* the point. I only ever want to think of Brad and Angelina that way, and you should too. That's the way it's supposed to be, because no one else really holds up to that yardstick.

Homosexual sex is *so* often discussed: "I just don't get why you would like that, it's so disgusting, who does what ... where?" But so many shades of black, white, ... and need I say *gray* exist in hetero camp that are hard to understand, I don't even know where to start. Some outlandish heterosexual acts have nearly scarred my unsuspecting retinae into celibacy.

We have not made enough progress when gays and lesbians have to prove that we aren't perverts or sexual deviants who are unfit to adopt our own children until proven otherwise simply because we're gay.

This doesn't just happen in "other places"; it happened to us even in "gay friendly" Seattle, in 2013! Every comment, slander, or open-minded word a person utters colors the places we live. Though it can seem we are all very separate, our lives all connect in unexpected ways.

My wife Nicole and I planned for our child together—conception to birth. She was with me from the moment she first encouraged me to have the baby in the first place, through interminable doctor's appointments and hormone injections, to reading me the stick that finally formed a plus. (Which she read while I hid my head in the other room to avoid seeing another failed attempt.) Then through the morning sickness, many waddling comforting walks, many trips to the store for yet more watermelon, and my long, *long*, long delivery. My devoted wife never left my side. The only smudge in that beautiful experience was that she had to undergo the aforementioned social worker's assessment and approval to "qualify" to be the adoptive parent of our own son. I don't think I need to point out the ridiculousness of this by comparing intentional gay parenting to accidental teenage pregnancy or deadbeat fathers who are no more involved than our anonymous sperm donor was.

I was reminded of how far we have to go.

I have never gotten over the picture of the very kind social worker telling us that she thought this was unjust: uncomfortably stammering and shuffling her feet as she went through the motions, including having Nicole take and pass a background check proving she had never been convicted of perverted or illegal acts. Nonetheless, the investigation had to be done and the social worker's uncomfortable questions answered, at a considerable expense to us, in order to satisfy state law. All to show that Nicole was fit to be a parent to her wife's child.

So I overcame my fear of potentially offending those in the church by speaking out against institutions that continue to perpetuate that sort of treatment. I love so many who are members and find some way to love and accept me and my family despite belonging to a church that still condones and perpetuates discrimination. Many members have already grown out of these policies, but the church continues to teach them to children in church and reinforce them to members who generally want to be loving and kind. Many good members struggle with justifying staying in the church, as evidenced by the article in the Salt Lake Tribune entitled "In this new era of doubt, will a stronger Mormon faith emerge?" It seems there is a crisis of faith among many members of the LDS church, and for multiple reasons.

I greatly appreciate the values that I learned from attending the Mormon Church; they helped mold me into the person I am today. Thanks to these teachings, I tried since childhood to lead the most kind life that I can, though now the path is no longer dictated for me by a church. Because of them I learned to trust and to listen more closely to my intuition, "the still, small voice." And I still pray to a higher power for guidance with hard choices as I was taught when I was a Sunbeam in primary school.

On the down side, I would never have been so homophobic (against myself, as it twisted), had I not been taught by the church that homosexuality was a perversion, "an abomination." Discrimination wasn't part of my natural "I like you till you prove me wrong" personality. This dogma is inconsistent with the golden rule—with what a just and kind God would teach and do. Yes, I would have thought homosexuality or trans-sexuality was hella weird or curious, but I would not have developed the condemning judgment I did without the church's influence. I was devastated and loathed myself when I realized I was gay, and I was as innocent as a baby white lamb at the time.

Not to mention so many of my Mormon friends were mildly to extremely repulsed by me, asking if I had "checked them out" while they were getting dressed and saying they didn't want me to stay at their houses—especially if there were young siblings there. It still makes me shudder that these family friends—my best friends through school—thought I was a perverted threat because of what they were taught at our church.

CHAPTER 3

A MORMON FLUNK

I knew I was different growing up.

As bitty, Mormon, clean slates, we are taught in sunday school that the Latter Day Saints are different. We follow different rules, we dress differently, we have a certain code of conduct. (We can't drink coffee for the love of all that's frickin' holy!) And it does take a *lot* of doing (or more importantly, *abstaining,*) from doing things most people want to do to be a good Mormon. For that reason, it is "known" within the church that we are special, and will be rewarded in the afterlife for our behavior, if not this life as well.

We stand out in a crowd, like a couple of tall, white and blonde missionaries wearing white shirts and name badges in... well, ... anywhere outside of Utah and Scandinavia. (Mormons no longer have predominantly blonde hair and blue eyes, but the stereotype persists).

Having now lived away from the Utah motherland for 15 years, I'm frequently reminded that the rest of the on-looking world has a fascination for Mormon stories. I left, and forgot after a while that deep down, I'm still weird due to those cultured roots and who I am now. There are still things that creep up in my previously LDS brain that are *not* conscious choices.

For instance, after 10 years of living away from Utah, I was learning about the retirement benefits at a new job when this thought hopped from my deep, dank, mushroom-spawning subconscious: "Hmmm,

I don't need to invest too heavily in a 401-K right now—the second coming of Christ is supposed to happen soon, and I'll just wish I had kept it and spent the money on food storage or a bomb shelter before the shizzle hit the fan."

So there it is—I solved that allocation issue.

Financial irresponsibility is actually the furthest thing from the Mormon way. But I have heard the second coming of Christ and the end of the evil world as we know it prophesied since my infancy. These concepts were made so real in my mind that they still affect my day-to-day subconscious outlook if left unchecked.

It's so ingrained that no amount of cerebral Clorox or time away can stop it from rearing its ugly head. I don't even see it coming—it just lurks in the shadows and then, BAM! Out of the cobwebs from crazy-town, the thoughts I have but don't claim as mine. Pushy, brainwash-y imposter thoughts that don't ask permission to interrupt my conscious flow. I'm glad others can't hear my messy inside voice, or I fear I would be sequestered as a protege to the ranting bag lady you can smell from any part of my neighborhood, who stops traffic to bellow to unsuspecting drivers that she is destroying evil empires with her mind as you drive along in your stupid "go-wagons", and to watch out for the colored lights in the sky and "boo hags", cause they want to steal your mind. And for this sage advice, gimme some dollas. That's all you got? Psshhhhh.

No one can stop the leaky, accidental expression of what was infused from childhood, even if it's not something you agree with as you age and make your own choices. You can only hide the recurring thought, laugh about it, or try to assuage it into submission. Or re-evaluate which parts of it you will and will not embrace. Mormon practice has a great deal of intelligent design that I don't take for granted. I still pause to consider things such as the importance of disaster planning and earthquake preparedness, I just don't mention that Mormons link being prepared for the second coming of Christ, when the righteous shall be lifted off the earth while the evil burn below, then replaced to survive for a time until righteous community resources are restored. Fifteen years hence, I like to think that the righteous are the majority of us doing the best good that we can, and not the few who are good, **and** who are in a certain religion.

Anyway, this outside interest in Mormonism is repeatedly demonstrated not only by television shows and Broadway plays but also in conversations each time I meet someone who asks me where I'm from. Add the super scoop of sticky intrigue that being gay and (ex-)Mormon provides, and it's a spicy blockbuster pausing for repeated applause.

Don't get me wrong; I don't always mind.

"Oh, you're from Salt Lake City?"

"Yes, I was raised a Mormon."

I do sometimes welcome it as a mindless escape from awkward conversations at parties. It allows my brain to switch on auto-pilot, and I can perhaps even seem interesting while putting no sweaty-palmed effort or original thought into the conversation that ensues.

"No, I'm not practicing—I'm a *recovering* Mormon. M-wa-hahaa."

They laugh. It's entertaining.

"Did you ever go into one of their temples? I hear they don't let people in unless they have a special card and pajamas."

They are leaning in, engaged and interested.

"Yeah, the card bit is true. I rebelled before I got my card, so I only went in twice to a protected enclosure within the temple where they baptize for the dead. I was 12. But I didn't get the whole tour."

At this point my new acquaintances usually have looks on their faces like they are walking the line between wanting to ask more questions and not really knowing where "going too far" is. They consciously evaluate how many drinks they have had before speaking. They are also wondering actively if I am pulling their leg with the baptizing for the dead bit.

Then they look on expectantly, and with not just a *little* trepidation.

I can throw them a bone if the conversation is still serving us well. "Yes, they baptize dead souls who did not accept the church in this life, so it allows them to be baptized by proxy in the afterlife. Then they can still score Celestial kingdom-hood in the afterlife.

It's like a back-up plan (soul insurance) for the dead. We would go to a big hot tub–type structure in the center of 12 life-sized, carved granite oxen and literally be dunked for each name read out. The temple and the oxen were artistically stunning. It was weird, but beautiful."

"What's with the Oxen"?

"I think they represented the 12 tribes of Israel, but I couldn't swear by it."

Sometimes they stop there, or tell me that they were raised Episcopalian, or that their grandpa raised oxen when they were kids on a farm in the Midwest. To which I grasp for an appropriate response, conjure a courtesy laugh to follow, and linger until it's polite to go.

The best is a spirited, tipsy guy who's wife is not at the party and he doesn't have to drive home. He asks it all. Conspiratorially, with a sideways shiz-eating grin, he half whispers, "Is it true that you can't even have sex with the girl before you marry her? You just have to cross your fingers it's good?"

"I know, right? Talk about a gamble," I chortle back if he doesn't seem too dirt baggish about it.

Like I said, it can be a party favor. I don't always mind it.

"So, are you and your wife still practicing?"

This is a sincere and confused, but trying to be respectful, question of my favorite sort—typical of ever-P.C. Northwesterners. They don't look you directly in the eyes, as if to avoid inciting aggression if it's an off question (you know, like avoiding eye contact with foamy-mouthed dogs). They make caring, curious, and sincere gestures with sidelong, respectful glances—sans judgement, of course.

And how would they know otherwise? It's a rare, exotically odd religion. How would non-Mormons know that for someone in the church, it so laughably doesn't work without "the man heading the family and wife supporting?" The ability to breed little persons with all the easiest reproductive plumbing is the assumption without exception. The religion strictly prohibits the practice of same-sex marriage, or even same-sex impure thoughts for that matter. And even if I had *wanted* to continue with the Mormon system of beliefs, the church wouldn't have *let* me in a million years while having a female partner. In November 2015 the church publicly declared people married to same-sex partners "apostates" and banned even their children from baptism until they are 18 and willing and able to denounce their parents' "choice". An apostate, as defined by the Oxford dictionary is defined as: a person who renounces a religious or political belief or principle. In case there was any question of acceptance before, which there wasn't for those of us who were bearing our souls to our bishops weekly as we were searching for help in the process of figuring ourselves out.

So, due to Mormon fascination, we have the wildly popular musical *The Book of Mormon*, books like *Under the Banner of Heaven*, and TV shows like "Big Love." I'm sure I could think of more if I didn't live in a largely media-free cave. People crowd to watch these things— heck, I could barely get nose-bleed seats for year two of *The Book of Mormon* show in Seattle!

The idea of the church is indeed a delicacy of tantalizing practices that cannot be unveiled without some outside interest, fascination, or entertainment. However, I don't want this book to be a mockery of a religious belief system that so many people cherish (well, not in a way that's different than the way I gently mock everything equally). I think most members now days, despite the firm church standing on the subject, really do try to be as understanding as they can toward gay people. After the 2015 policy was announced, many members actually left the church in protest. Many others who are kind spirited toward gay people, meanwhile, still count themselves members in good standing. They don't want it in their families of course, but they're not mean-spirited and chasing LGBT people out of town with torches.

As a rule, they're friendly: always nice.

To everyone.

Which can be disorienting and scary for someone who's lived in a larger city—like there's an inside joke only you don't know it, and Ashton Kutcher is going to jump out from behind a Dan's Grocery shopping cart and punk you on television. (P.S. If you're ever in Utah shopping, and end up in a Dan's, save yourself 40 wasted minutes; they don't sell beer or alcohol of any kind. You didn't miss the aisle).

I want to give a positive view to you Mormons, or anyone in an unaccepting environment, who are as freaked out as I was about what's happening to them. And possibly shed some light on the good life for us that is out there. I want you to have another book on the shelf to consider reading when you insert "Gay and Mormon" in your online search. It seems right to present a more balanced picture—something from the other side. Something containing hope for your future.

For gay people raised Mormon, the next thing you may think that I once thought *myself* is: "You don't know what's going to happen in the afterlife—living happily isn't proof that you're right. It just proves you're doing what you want and you're happy in this life. And that doesn't mean much in the eternal scheme of things. It's not spiritual insurance." To that I would now answer that you'll just have to trust that peace will come to you in time, and you'll know it for yourself without a doubt. The church is based in large part on faith, so you may already have some practice! I propose you exercise faith in your own goodness and believe that you were made right. Don't listen to judgement from those who don't understand, and then make harsh decisions about your own worth. Trust in the example of my staunchly religious father's softened heart that people change and are realizing every day that the Source who made us all is made of *unconditional* love. The people that are worth having in your life will come around. If people are really trying to be uplifted and Christ-like, they do so by aligning with the intentions of that Godly Source. Anything but that perfect love is fraudulent.

There are many signs that will tell you what's right if you recognize your natural cues for connecting to God or your Source. Prayer or directed meditation is the most important tool to employ. It can buoy you up during and after a departure from the church, when you often need it most. Spirit speaks up in silence and can't be heard over the roar of fear, so offer an open and clear channel in your head from time to time if you can manage it. My mental picture of whom I was praying to changed significantly, but the feeling I got from praying to a power larger than myself only got stronger. As a reply to my prayers, this feeling let me know whether my path was right or wrong, helping me to make some of my life's harder choices. And it let me know I was always worthy of love even when I made the most craptastic choices anyway. Which was a lot, despite knowing better. Many people have built their lives on, and still appreciate, Mormon values and live honest, free and fulfilling lives with a same-sex partner. There are so many options for life out there, including varying degrees of religion, that can bring incredible joy. I don't mean the shallow, this-world-only, partial joy that comes from thinking "my marriage is not as good as hetero-marriage, but it's ok." I mean the real thing—all-the-way-to-your-bones joy. A joy so deep you don't have to ask yourself, "Am I really going to hell after this is said and done?" anymore. You just choose your own way to live.

Don't believe that you don't amount to as much as they do—that you don't deserve to be as happy as heterosexual people because you choose to embrace the way you were made, and love someone sincerely, who is of the same sex.

The most significant thing I discovered that finally helped me scrape up some love for myself, is the knowledge that God is not performing a loyalty test on us. He does not intend to judge us harshly by sending us to harrowing nether-kingdoms of regret because we loved the people we fell in love with on this planet. Someone that you came primed and predestined to love. No God worth His or Her salt would do that.

Would you do that to your own child, sibling or friend?

If there's anything I believe, it's that current church policy on the treatment of gay people who love and live with a partner does not follow the intended spirit of God's law. Yes, LDS church leaders are kind in statement, and released a letter recently with some touching gestures. They discourage hateful or violent behavior toward LGBT (lesbian, gay, bisexual, transgendered, or queer) individuals, but it doesn't change the facts. We are not allowed in the church because they believe there is something inherently wrong with us. For a church to presume to know what God would do, and know the hearts of those involved in same sex relationships, is impossible. And then to reject the children of the believed transgressors, is deeply damaging to those people who now believe they are cursed, or not worthy of God's blessing of the church. It's damaging as well to those members who believe that now, it's ok to judge others because their church does. It's damaging to the families of LGBT people who, in their belief systems, can't make heads or tails of how to think of their now ousted child or sibling. Many emotionally flip-flop between mistrust in a religion who would judge their child this way, then careen back to suffer deep disappointment in their child who was too weak to "choose the right". They often wonder "what did I do wrong?" It's a ripple effect of negativity all caused by undue judgment. We are not equipped to judge each other, because we haven't walked in their shoes. We're not supposed to judge each other. One of the biblical quotes that seems to be consistent with a loving God is John 8:7 where Jesus finds a mob eager to execute a woman caught in adultery. He stopped them by asking that the one with no sin in their life should step forward and throw the first stone. Glass houses, y'all. God is good, and not obligated to uphold man's flawed interpretation of his laws.

Church policies that outlaw LGBTs from fully practicing in the church are often biblically misinterpreted, warping the true intent of God through serpentine assumptions and translations. If you are that person and in the Mormon Church, don't take mistranslations into your heart or believe you are deserving of lesser salvation and/ or lovelessness in this life. Believe that most of your families, even the most recalcitrant, will come around, enough to find a way to understand you and keep you in their lives. They won't always accept your partner with open arms—they might never be very comfortable with that. Or someday they may like your partner more than they like you, as in my case. Know that if they don't, there are often "adoptive" friend-families who serve as true families (thus the gay phrase, "Are they family?" which is equivalent to, "Are they gay?" When I first heard this slang, I was incredulous that there were so many siblings in a family that were gay till someone filled me in on the lingo). You can have friend-families who act like real, tight-knit families; it's common for these relationships to last a lifetime and fill some of the voids of familial relationships, as so many gay people share the experience of having been rejected by their families of origin. Though the tragic pain of being ostracized by your given family always remains, it says more about your family than it does about you if they never come around.

Know it gets better! And you aren't alone.

If you're the parent or in some way related to someone who is coming out, know that any caring expression, even if you aren't elated with all they do or how they do it, is meaningful to him or her. They're in your life for a reason. They are special, different, and strong spirits finding their way. Don't leave them to wonder if you care.

In considering why I wanted to write this book, the reason that kept calling me back from self-conscious high-tailing was that I needed to read this when I was figuring myself out. I know that I would have eaten it up when I had a thirst for a new perspective and more objective, inspiring information. When I went searching for an example or barometer of normal, the "Born that way" book's perspective was all I could find in the dark ages before widespread, gloriously anonymous internet. There still isn't too much information available for Mormon "others" that has a positive, God-*trusting*, nonjudgmental view and offers hope for us borne from this religion that I've seen.

Even though "born that way" sounds like a story of someone who was born homosexual and is therefore expressing a natural trait, in reality, the book incites deep shame in gay readers for what they naturally are. It encourages them into thinking they should will themselves into heterosexuality or lonely celibacy. It was all I found when searching for help; a "Fix what's wrong with you" anthem implying you should overcome your deplorable nature. It encourages subservience to harsh Mormon doctrines and asks you to sacrifice your nature and ultimate happiness to be in accord with current Mormon doctrine, outlining how and why you should deny who you are and whom you love. To me, "born that way" sounded like an overture to flying my self-loathing kite in the religious, heterosexual-steeped wind.

This phase of "fixing" is like step one in an addiction program: "Admit you have a problem."

The next step the church proposes in the "fixing" process is, "Prove your strength and devotion to God and His plan by denying what you are and whom you want to give love to. (It's a problem: Not a life option).

Next: Sink the fading self-loathing kite into shredding brambles to die a bloody, muscle-twitching, afterlife-bonus-earning and righteous death." Live without the joys of a life partner for whom you care, and do it for God and afterlife rewards. (Bury your hope for love in this life forever, queers).

It sounds silly, but these were the options I had to consider in deciding to live the way I was. It took me years of deliberation to sort out that I wasn't just *trying* to hear what I wanted to hear, choosing the "easy" way of doing what I was born wanting to do, but to really believe that it was *more* right for me to love a woman than a man. That's why I was born with aligned attractions to a woman. Duh.

What I needed was an example of what gay *really* was from someone who knew where I was coming from; I needed some Mormon mental recovery. I needed to realize that LGBTs are just regular old people taking out their trash on Wednesdays and struggling to pay bills, with some days full of love and some days full of stress and struggle—that in relationships, they take on this struggle together just like all the straights I had been raised to know. No, we don't all rove around gay bars every night, affording strippers their living wage, contracting diseases in dark alleys and gnarly bathrooms, or—whatever other skanky black leather scary scenario was in that crazy head of mine when I thought of the evil of "other" life. I needed to see what LGBTs' way of life was really like—not the ungodly horrors I cooked up in my unexposed, rattled head. Nice same-sexed people who just love and support each other, and go through the same common things that most couples do.

CHAPTER 4

THE SPECIAL GAY NETHER-KINGDOM TO COME

I felt like the only homo abnormality alive in the isolated, warp-world of Salt Lake City, Utah. I was confused, because I didn't see myself in the mannish camp of lady gays that I had met (all 2 of them) by the time I was 15. Nor, for that matter, did I identify as a straight woman or a "lipstick lesbian." Nothing fit. I just continued to feel miserably awkward. I thought I *could* be bisexual, still clinging like a codependent Koala to a desperate hope of normalcy someday. After all, how can you rule out a person whom you haven't met yet?

I know there is love to be had in every camp, but it wasn't *my* camp, and I felt estranged from every category. For example, lesbians. For the love of Dog (true Mo swear there), what a horrible word: lesbian. It even *sounds* like an affliction you catch by being careless around third-world toilet seats. I couldn't identify with anything on this front because I didn't even know what it was to *be* that. I was very lucky to have some amazing, straight adult friends I worked with who I told about the "gay scare" as I called it, and were a very loving and supportive orthodontic office gaggle. They gave me some hope that I could find my place somewhere, all of us laughing that it sure as hell-o wasn't in Utah, as I recounted my dates and disastrous forays into the one and only lesbian bar in town. Their support, and being able to laugh at the scary craziness of my life at the time was priceless.

There are plenty of amazing public role models now, thankfully. For gays or bisexuals there is an Anderson Cooper, Ellen DeGeneres, Michael Sam, Jodie Foster, Dan Savage, Ellen Page or Channing Tatum for all seekers out there, who can uplift them to the lofty heights of gay okayness. As for those pushing oppressive gender boundaries, there is Jaden Smith, Lady Gaga, Ruby Rose, RuPaul, and Eddie Izzard. But as we all like to recognize someone socially visible outside ourselves who is representative of us, either by sexuality, race, gender, or religion, I fear that no one in the Osmond family is heading out of the closet soon. With the exception of the amazing and articulate Martha Beck, I haven't heard stories of many others who underwent the Mormon brand of spiritual distress, believing in the church they were taught to believe in from a tender age, and then having to make one of these choices (or what I thought were these choices):

1. **You live man's interpretation of God's law, no matter your inclinations.** This life is a test: the Olympics of Spiritual Self-Control. Are you going to be a good, golden sheep in the fold? If you were born a gay wad, or a black person before 1978, you just needed more of a challenge from God, and you should rise to rally. If you tough it out through the blink of an eye that is this life, you will be rewarded richly forever and all eternity. Amen.

Behind door number 2: You forsake your eternal place with God, and your forever sealed secular family, to be happy in this life. You are a shallow, shortsighted glutton of meaningless, sweaty sex and sinning. Not to be rude or anything, but your potential to be God and Goddess yourself is now swept away, because the person who kisses you goodnight and proffers the other good things of relationships is fleeting or trifling. Holding hands while walking, unfolding our enlightening conversations about life, hugs after a hard day, encouragement to grow and test your limits to become your best, laughing at your children together as they do their crazy baby stuff (poop on the floor and fingerprint the walls with it, barf on strangers on an airplane, imitate parental eccentricities, etc)—if you choose these things, you will not go to heaven when you die. In short, you seek and find the life most everyone, gay or straight, wants (with or without the baby stuff), but you give up eternal salvation.

Make this shortsighted choice, and, according to the church, you had better enjoy this life now, because regret will be your ever-loving afterlife companion in hell, my friend. You'll remember the choice you made for that warm partnership, and you'll live the rest of eternity in the nether kingdoms gnashing your teeth, knowing your choice cost you your goodie bag of forever fulfillment. But if you want to do that, go ahead. You have free choice. God gives you free choice and then finds the worthy according to what you do with it. So goes the logic of man-made rules, anyway.

After years of being a little fearful of others not like me (like I was an unwanted imposter who could be ousted at any time), I learned to accept that most people who judge only do so because they just don't understand or were taught it was bad and believe what they were taught. I can't hold a little bit of initial homophobia against those who have never had cause to think twice about it. I myself was a homophobic son of a gun at the time I realized, "Oh, shiz, I am one of those." I repelled myself; it had been so ingrained in me. I never had a reason to question the truth of what I had been taught about gays, just like I didn't question what I was told would happen if I ran into a scorpion in a dark corner barefoot. My dad told me I would get hurt if I went off the neighborhood jump on my craptastic bike like the other kids were doing, and when I did it anyway I removed the flesh from all my pointed parts very painfully and dramatically. Not to say I became totally obedient, I sure as shootin' did not. But I did learn not to have to test every little thing my parents and teachers were very clear in warning me about. Why would I bother forming a different opinion about queers and gays unless incited to for a compelling reason?

We all wall off in our own ways to find our safe havens. We keep the Unknowns and the monsters out, to keep an easy groove going that doesn't require maintenance and frequent re-examination. It's how our brains allow us to get through life without becoming stressed out, having to ever-mutate and reinvent the wheel.

All of these confused, unsure reactions to people we don't yet understand are not only forgivable, but predictable and totally reversible with a few curiousity driven questions—if one takes the time to ask. Some people cross a line and are actively and creatively cruel and inhuman. Not to be childish, but they should probably be destroyed in a fiery ball of painful transitional role play, or therapy, or both. It's usually only the scarred, deep and creepy Jeffrey Dahmers, or closeted gays in angry, reactive denial, who get that mean. That being said, there are a lot of us being hurt out there, and not a lot of serial killers, so.... some work to be done.

I was once beaten up by a guy who came to a **known** gay bar and hit on me. I politely said I had a girlfriend, but thanks anyway and have a good night. (I was confused, as it was not a mystery that this bar was *gaaaayyyyy*, but I was quizzically polite anyway.) Later that night, he waited for me out in the parking lot to share with me his feelings on the matter. I know people acting violently are usually the exceptions, but it's still all too common. Many people who are anything other than heterosexual suffer violent acts against them just for existing as they are, ranging from minor bullying to severe physical assault ending in death. Sometimes the offender is a gay person made to feel so ashamed of themselves that they hurt others like them, hating themselves so much they think an act of violence will change them- or at least the perception others have of them. No matter the perpetrator, it leaves a victim with a residual fear that takes great effort to overcome.

There are some undeniably different things about the Mormon Church that I'm repeatedly asked about. Even those in the church must understand the fascination, and I hope they will excuse me for addressing some of the more interesting tenets; it's done without malevolence. I have replaced my once reflexive disdain of the church with a little, I hope, tasteful and caring humor to enlighten and entertain the always curious and inquisitive folks who ask me once they find out I was "one of them".

If you are a member of the church and still reading, I hope we can land on a common ground. I hope to offer insights that can help you understand more fully "others" who are just outside the norm—and the difficult path many of us have taken to be able to love ourselves. Life is a call for unrepressed laughter at human nature, the way we all land on beliefs and ideas that can be comforting and convoluted all at once. I'd also like to ask the church to soften its stance; it has already shown a kinder and more accepting approach to the embarrassed gay confessor who wants to stay in the church. But the proclamation made November 5, 2015, was harsh. I dare to hope for another look at the *spirit* behind the ostracizing laws laid down that day.

Anyhoo.... we all want things. I won't hold my breath.

Back to the questions about Mormonism I'm most commonly asked:

- There *is* an undergarment (sacreligiously dubbed "magic jammies" by sassy young saints) worn by each worthy Mormon after going to the temple at the appropriate age and if living in consistency with the Mormon standard. You have to have a "temple recommend" from your Bishop and a card to get in. The garments have meaningful symbols stitched within them that proffer spiritual protection for the wearer. This is why it's recommended to wear them *always*. There is an old folk story that tells the story of a young man who was tempted to go swimming in a member's pool while on his mission, a known no-no. He was somewhere hot and he rationalized it was ok, despite Satan's increased interest in bringing down those young men when out delivering the true gospel to the world. The overheated missionary disregarded the rule, and as he was hurtling toward the water from his bounding jump from the springboard, onlookers saw a streaming expulsion of blood spread from his body to the lapping waves at the pool's edge when he hit the water. He had a large, unexplained gash on his chest when he was later fished out of the bloody water. Nearly drowned and desperately sputtering, he was wholly unable to explain what had happened. There was no flotating knife arranged just

29

so, or bobbing razor blades spread out for a hapless diver to meet on investigation of the pool after the incident. In the end it was just a hard lesson about disobedience and a head scratching mystery of quantum physics. Anyway, back to topic. These garments are sacred and said to be blessed; I was told that they are made only by LDS members and are meant to constantly remind wearers of their covenants as well as to protect them.

- Caffeine is strongly forbidden. However, many a Mormon drinks a Diet Coke with relish and is not ousted from the ranks. This is a strong recommendation in the LDS Word of Wisdom, but not an absolute no-no.

- Alcohol is prohibited. All of it. Even if you mix it with something wholesome like a virgin goat's raw magic milk. No booze whatsoever. Yes, even on New Year's Eve.

- Premarital sex is not allowed. Yes even that kind. All kinds—let's not get graphic. Yes, no special exceptions on your birthday, or if you just got engaged. Even over the pants action is discouraged. Yes, really. This deserves special attention, because, Jeez, it sucks, and you do marry blind. Let's give credit where credit is due for those young saints who stick it out. I mean don't.

- Members must wear modest clothing without exposing the aforementioned undergarment. No tank tops, short shorts, string dresses, etc. Again, loads of respect for members here. Utah summers are hotter than Hades.

These things are *all* real rules and recommendations—current standards that are actually practiced by those in the Church of Jesus Christ of Latter Day Saints. (This is the full name of the church. "Mormon" is a nickname. The *Book of Mormon* is their own official book of doctrine, read today just as it was said to be received and translated by Joseph Smith, the founder. And who doesn't need a nickname with a name that long?

Alternately, these things are **not true:**

- As a rule, Mormons don't make their own clothes.
- They don't wear their hair in buns. Or wholesome braids. (Specifically, SLC mo's wear their hair a little too big, armed with hairspray and ratting, but not quite 80s-big. Still, it can be a *little too much.* I have an old friend who actually wears a hairpiece. She says it's because her hair is a little thin, but it's not. She's just from a small town in Utah, where hair feels better when it's bigger.
- They don't grow all their own food. They buy their food from the grocery store. Though growing your own food in gardens and general self-sufficiency are encouraged, they are not expected to feed a family of 8 from the back yard. Or 10, which is better.
- They don't practice polygamy, and the thought of doing so is grody (at least among most LDS women) and not encouraged or talked about much. Polygamy is a vestigial practice having been disavowed in 1890 by president Wilford Woodruff. They felt it was needed in the early days of the church because they needed to repopulate within the church and there were many more women than men. After much discord with the US government, they gave the manifesto that they no longer condoned plural marriage, but some continued to practice polygamy and became their own separate faction called fundamentalists. Most women in the church now would have men talking to the hand, exclaiming "Ugh, *heck* no," if the brothers even brought it up, likely having a bed to themselves for a time just for asking.
- They don't have horns that recede with any phase of the moon. No horns. I don't know where that one comes from, but more than twice I have been asked about the presence of horns on Mormons. Yup, really.
- They don't wear their garments every single minute of every single day. Members I've known do take off the "magic

jammies" to make them babies, not just to shower or swim, contrary to popular folklore. I can't speak for all, but most modern Mo's don't just work around the slits. This is a very common creepy question, believe it or not, and not always from the drunk guy.

What else? I want to cover all the usual burning questions and get on with it. Yes, young Mormon men are *strongly* encouraged at 18 to go on a mission. By encouraged, I mean sort of shamed and moderately ostracized for not going. (I do know one guy who's mom was sick. He was nobly taking care of her and was excused from serving a mission). Mormon women can serve missions if they want to, but they have to wait until the ripe old age of 21 if they've failed to marry by that time. There might be a disproportionately high number of lesbos serving those missions. Can't prove it, just sayin'.

CHAPTER 5

7.5 ON THE "HOW MORMON?" SCALE

I grew up in a pretty strongly Mormon home. There is every brand of Mormon, just like in any religion, I imagine. "A lazy Catholic" comes to mind; this is the "Jack Mormon" equivalent of our breed: talking the talk on Sundays, but walking another walk entirely on the sly. There are those who practice in the LDS church because it's their culture. But do they really buy the whole three levels of afterlife—the concept that you have a qualifying round before you go to heaven—when the doctrine is more closely inspected? Doubtful. If they had been born with any other religion dominating their schools and neighborhoods, they wouldn't have left the comfort of their lives to seek out the spiritual depths of the Mormon gospel.

There are the kind, sweet people who *happen* to be Mormon and naturally live what the religion preaches, but not letter-of-the-law people. My mom is like this. She lives fully in the church, with good intentions and a kind core; she is a very active member to this day. After a couple divorces (not Mormon kosher), she suffered the wrath of social and self-judgment and some very cold shoulders. This, interestingly enough, drew her deeper into the church (if it burns when you touch it, touch it longer! Just kidding, mom). She thought she needed to live better and the rest would follow, and her faith that God will work out the details in the end is a strong and admirable faith.

Then there are the die-hards. My father was a very strict follower of the church. A letter-of-the-law kind of guy, who kept track of the chips earned and chips doled out, with just a little fire and brimstone. A "scare-you-straight" undercurrent, but a genuinely nice guy. He would tell you so. In his spare time, he read complex volumes on the details of Mormon doctrine that could substitute for baby booster seats at the dinner table.

I believed what I was told about the church from the time I was a wee one (as if it occurs to a child that there is a choice). I think I had a tendency toward spirituality anyway, and Mormonism was a stage on which to build that quality and expand it. There were *more* strict Mormon homes than ours, to be sure. Yes, my dad was cuckoo for the intellectually detailed doctrine, but he was still pretty cool about day-to-day stuff, and he was usually fun to be with and laid back. After I was 11 and my parents divorced, he wasn't around very often, and we were exposed much less to his exacting LDS viewpoint. Still, the major teachings of the church, and its encouragement to live worthy of having the spirit with us, remained. We were taught since toddling always to show God that we were following His light by doing what he said.

For example, when I was seven years old, soon to be eight (the age when a young member is baptized into the church), my brother was chasing me around the house, whipping me with a dish towel. I did all I could to get away, half fighting and half playing with that crazed kid laugh/scream rattling the house. My mom was in the other room doing something as we tore through the house, being much rowdier than usual. I jumped up on a little coffee table after being chased into a corner, and to avoid another snap, I jumped into the air, planning to land on the edges of the hexagonal glass topped table. Bright, right? Well, of course, three snaps of the dishtowel later, my bare right foot crushed the unforgiving glass. This didn't bother me at all until I landed on the shattered bits of insulted sharp remnants, then the top shards shook and fell inward to join them, cutting both my legs badly on the way to their rest. My leg looked like a Vampire's dream, with rivulets of blood from multiple cuts and punctures from my knees down. I quickly swallowed my screams, knowing:

1. I was dead meat for breaking our nice table.
2. I was unworthy. I had just failed a test.

I felt so ashamed. I was to be baptized next week and this was my behavior? My parents didn't have the money to get us sewn up in the E.R. every time we mangled each other. How was I going to stand in that holy water with my leg filleted like a halibut? I should have known better. I flogged myself, knowing that this wouldn't have happened if I had listened to the spirit, the "still small voice" that would have protected me if I had been more in tune. I blubbered to my mom, who was busy applying pressure to and bandaging her hot mess sniffling on the blue toilet seat in our bathroom, that my leg didn't hurt as badly as it hurt inside, because I knew I had done wrong. I was seven years old! The scar on my right foot looked just like a check mark, and I remembered looking at it after the fact, thinking that God had put a visible demerit mark there to help me remember how it felt to fail and to remind me to do His will next time.

Guilt much?

So in a nutshell, I'm telling you this Mormon story having come from a churchy home of say 7.5 on a scale of 1 to 10. –1 being equivalent to a roving savage, 10 being the Doctrine-thumping, can't-sit-next-to-a-stranger-on-an-airplane-without-a-full-blown-effort-at-conversion type.

We were a very closed cultural group in the 'burbs of Utah. I remember knowing very few people at all who weren't in the ward. (These are names of particular church sections, based solely on location around the church building.) The general sense among neighbors was an overwhelming sadness for them. The empties, the hope-not heavies of heart. The outside others. They were lacking so, so much—broken and retarded in spiritual growth and expansion. We were taught that we were the blessed, so the fact that they didn't have what we did was so sad. We were supposed to be a humble people, but there was a fair amount of pride in being a chosen LDS person keeping the faith. We had, after all, done something right in heaven to be born in this ideal position in this life after all. And boy, they really had it coming in the afterlife if they didn't get it together. I later got to know this non-Mormon family in the neighborhood, and remember being genuinely shocked to find how much I liked them. They were nice and rode bikes, not brooms, and had to go in for early dinner just like us. I don't know what I expected; I just thought they would be *so* different. Wear funny capes, have black lights and red carpet, eat raw meat. But they were disturbingly normal.

I thought, "Why doesn't someone just tell them, and they can be with *us?*"

I asked my father as much.

"They had their chance and blew it," he said, only half joking. After a sideways, arched-eyebrow glance from my mother, he revised: "Well, honey, don't repeat that. They have heard about the gospel, but they just haven't chosen the right path yet. Maybe if you're a great example to them, their kids will see the light. Why don't you invite them to Sunday school, and share with them your testimony of the gospel?"

Chapter 6

Closet Cases

In retrospect, what would have helped me the most was knowing a real, out and proud, "normal-ish" couple when I was on the cusp of my outing. I felt so miserably awkward and "different" inside without knowing why. Yes, I was gay and didn't get it yet, but many tweens feel awkward for one self-conscious reason or another—zits, hormone swings, unwanted erections, etc. Junior high school is fitting punishment for the scum of humanity! In reality, I fit in just fine in my gawky, low-confidence teenaged normalness. That is, until I had a glimmer of the yet unknown "abnormal" in me. I then assumed I wasn't worthy of fitting in anymore, let alone being one of the cool kids, and I missed opportunities by ostracizing myself in a big way.

If I could have just had a glimpse of a happily religious or ex-Mormon with good values, proudly living with her same-sex spouse they loved and cherished, I could have seen there was no need for shame, and more easily conjured up the faith that things could work out for me too. I needed a visual to get my hopes up and give me forward momentum toward embracing my true self. There was no inspiring program like "It Gets Better," created by Dan Savage and his partner. Talk about old school: We didn't even have the Internet my first years of college! Like me, many LGBTs don't stay in heavily religious areas like Utah and Idaho, or they keep their nature apologetically quiet due to the overlying cultural climate that the religion creates. It makes it harder to live comfortably when feeling like you're outside the cultural norm looking in. So, of course, many leave as soon as they can.

For all these reasons there weren't many gays to relate to back then that I could see. And even though the dark ages are over, and every kid can access gay-related information on the Internet, it's not quite the same as knowing one in person: an uncle or a teacher or a neighbor who is real and whom you can talk to. I still would have struggled greatly, but it would have been easier without a blind goal at the end. I couldn't equate the "boring," book-reading, Vanilla, geeky me with the gay idea I had in my head from the two men I had once seen on television and my gym teacher. Figuring it out alone with all my infused shame and doubt was demoralizing and had me truly fearing for my everlasting soul when I someday died. I wondered what I had done wrong to deserve this sickness.

I would have loved to stop caring what someone else thought my pants, my skirt, my short hair, my athletic inclinations, or my tinted Chapstick *really* meant. Why the heck does all of that matter? Our relationships matter, not all the characterizations around the way we look (unless a gay couple wears the same thing at the same time—a prosecutable crime. Swing and a miss, people. Even fashion-free lesbos should know better). Trying to fit or *not* fit a stereotype is exhausting. All beautiful, unstereotypable types come in all different packages, as we all know from quippy posters and perky ads that annoy most of us. But it is sometimes true, and to all you queers and "others" in Utah or the cultural equivalent:

You are the definition of *extraordinary*. Your life is no longer as predictable as you once thought; you're not a production line cut-out, and you will be pushed to find your new mold. If you don't see the extraordinary in yourself right now, then keep at it. I won't lie this may not feel like a gift for a long time, so hang in there! What better way to build your character and shape your life more genuinely and completely than figuring out that you are so very different (in a way) than most of the people around you? I urge you to remember this, even when:

Parents feign lack of disappointment (if they're worth a nickel).

Friends can gasp and wonder how many times, disgusted, they changed clothes in front of you.

You're judged, ostracized, excommunicated.

You're kicked out of your home, or even physically abused.

You often really don't even want to *be you*, yourself. I mean, now you have to sort out a whole new idea of life and the way it will look. Some young people have good LGBT examples to follow, or a very strong character, but many have no examples, don't have the confidence yet, and don't know how to get what they need. So that picture is hazy, and many grasp fitfully in the dark for anything close. Or anyone.

This is the heart of the matter, unfortunately. We often start from behind, unless we are that rare species of confident, early bloomer. As young adults figuring out relationships, it can get messy going through emotions now that most heteros usually tried on in early puberty or sooner. (Real jealousy! *This* is what they were feeling? No wonder they acted a fool!)

Young LGBTs who come out in a non-nurturing environment have to rethink and reconfigure themselves, often from scratch, at the age where they finally figure out that they're different. This is hard! But to look ahead to the positive, it also opens the opportunity, if done right, to really be the most authentic you that you can be. You don't have to reflexively live up to a father or mother's expectations. You might abandon any other predicated assumptions that just don't fit you anymore. Someone who does this and applies it to his life across the board can readily become the definition of a leader, an innovator, and a strong-willed, authentic person—someone to be reckoned with. By dealing with the deck you were dealt in a positive way, you can develop the qualities that will help you come out ahead in every category of life.

Be honest with yourself about what you really want for your happiness. Start working toward it no matter what others think and find a way to love this wreck that may seem like you right now. Be inspired; you have reason to feel optimistic!

Then get out from behind—to the front—where you will belong after your inner work and growth has been achieved. After all the growth you've been through, gaining skills and confidence in the face of resistance, when you're done pushing through you should arrive ahead! Represent your inspired LGBT self proudly, knowing most of your peers don't have to go through these rigors, so don't gain the character you do, going through what you have. The awkwardness and self-doubt gather dust and start to swirl behind your fast-moving feet as you leave those burdensome emotions behind. Don't let them—or most importantly, don't let you—put Baby in a corner. (Yes, I'm old, but it remains one of the best movie quotes of all time by Mr. Swayze—just watch the movie.)

What other experience has the potential to create an open, adventurous, and persevering soul who is at peace with her life's direction because she had to take the bull by the horns, figuring out piece by piece what she is about, and where she would place those pieces? Often realizing, these people may not like me anymore. Then what? How do I move on? Many heterosexuals follow the status quo without having to go through the equivalent emotional and spiritual challenges. In contrast, overcoming the obstacles set for gays sets a stage for greatness.

If the challenge is too great, however, if the surroundings are too constrictive, or if a gay person is just raised in the wrong place at the wrong time, we end up with tragedy. At worst there are suicides—desperate kids who had thrived with opportunity in childhood but for a variety of reasons end up unable to deal with the idea of living life as they are anymore. Another frequently seen outcome is becoming a substance abusing vacuum of the person they could have been in attempt to dampen negative emotions about who they are and what they are worth. The other most common is the closet case, a fake-it-till-you-make-it attempt to hide behind unfulfilling, dishonest heterosexual marriages.

Simply having more LGBT people out there living proudly really does make all the difference in the world to those in their formative years. This influence also changes peers who can make the lives of gay teens so interminably hard. I can't count how many people have told me their families came around or softened, after having watched Ellen's show for years and having a kind and likable face to put to the gay label. Ok, I can count, but it takes both hands. Ellen's struggle wasn't an easy one- she had real and publically visible losses. But her courage to do it anyway was more far-reaching in it's effect than I'm sure she could have fathomed. My good friend's ancient, conservative grandmother told her that if she (Ellen) was "such a good gal—I see her on TV, and ya know she's nothing strange and just a positive, funny lady," then maybe it wasn't so bad that her granddaughter was "a gay." I keep using Ellen as an example, because I don't get out much, though now there are many out there. Michael Sam, bless your bold, Texan heart for coming out in the macho world of football. How difficult it must have been for you, but how very influential it was for so many who watched as you spoke your truth.

Celebrity advice and inspiration, with a willingness to stand out, is priceless. Having someone admirable show that the negative elements about gays preached in a church or yelled in a schoolyard are untrue is essential for all of us to move forward. As a young adult, I needed to see that two men or women together didn't create a strange repeating stutter of gender tendencies, tripping redundantly over each other. I needed examples that proved that I didn't have to give up family and live my life as a spectacle by being out. To see instead that gayness is just as intricate, interesting, beautiful, and synergistic combination as Brangelina (well, perhaps not as beautiful, even on a very good hair day, but let a girl dream). By the way, what a pair of amazing, bad-arse (yes, Mormon swear favorite) allies. Thanks to Brad Pitt and Angelina Jolie both for making public their intention to hold off on taking their marriage vows until gay marriage was legal for all—out of respect for *our* rights. I was impressed by that gesture of awareness.

I believe now that if there is a God of any kind who gives a hoot about these offspring She/He heaved through the atmosphere to earth, there is no way He/She would curse their kids with LGBT-ness, then blame them for their curse, and punish them forever and ever. It smells of utter bullshift. It's decisively contrary to what Christ taught, Godliness, or even a mere mortal parent worth a dime. I know a great number of kind, LDS people also believe this to some degree. To quote my mom: "I just have to have faith that He will make it all right in the end," despite the continued church stance that it is sinful behavior. This is my opinion, and there may be many variations of this for every LGBT Mormon or person coming to terms. My opinions and my understanding of my own connection to a higher power have evolved and changed over my lifetime, but this truth has consistently come to the surface clearly for me when it mattered most. It helped me make my best decisions, so I want to at least share it here with anyone who needs convincing: You are *naturally* worthy of love. You are made in the image of your Source; a God that isn't constricted by our mortal understanding of gender and earthly judgment. And you weren't born with a deficit to test.

I think I knew it deep down as the tormented baby budding gay-wad that I was, but not with enough confidence to skip over the dark times. I still believed in an archaic, thunderbolt-wielding, judgmental God. In time—a painfully long time—I learned to love myself by learning that the way I loved others was not only ok, but it was beautiful in it's difference. A love that was genuine, and strong enough to overcome my need for acceptance or approval by everyone I had ever cared about. That's a big, undeniable love.

In retrospect, that is some kind of force, right? If I had known the happy me 20 years ahead, I would have been less apologetic for just being me, and I would have been willing to try for more in life, as I hope you will. I really could have wasted much less time on low self esteem and hiding who I was and the talents I *did* have, because I didn't feel equal to or appreciated by the world, or at least the culture of my home. And because I escorted myself out of the mainstream—because I thought they didn't understand me (I was also reactive and didn't want to ask their permission anymore)—I quit trying, and it was harder to be myself in regular circles of regular people.

Which is what I am, and where I belong: with the regular-old, nothing crazy, day-in-day-out people, just trying to be the best they can. Regular people, who are sometimes tenacious and great, who sometimes fall flat on their faces after trying and failing, who are sometimes lazy and lame, and hope to come out just a little better today than the day before. I share in the high and low life cycles that most people go through. I don't have a special cult life that excludes me from the mainstream because I am a woman and I love one.

I was 18 when I isolated myself. I became a self-prescribed pariah and did myself a disservice, hiding in my crazy unnecessary shame. I spent my time mainly with other lost and young LGBTs, staying out late and trying things on for size that I knew didn't fit me. This I did not always do with elegance or grace. In fact, I was a stellar jackwagon on a few occasions that prompted me to quit it all for a few months here and there.... I kept going to school and worked hard, but I didn't find my best self in some of those late nights or in some relationships I chose. I didn't have the confidence to be myself in the regular world for many years. If you are in this boat, please inject the knowledge into your mind that you *can* surf over that sad and unnecessary way of dealing with coming out, and just cultivate the person you are naturally. Look the self in the eye that you're trying to numb out, and get to know his or her greatness instead of drowning out what "everyone will think. It only matters what *you* think of you in the long run.

The experience can make you gritty; it digs your stubborn, gay feet in and makes you gain the strength of character you need if you want to come out of that scare all right. My younger sister has also come out of the closet in Utah recently, and I should include that her experience was not nearly as negative as mine was. People were kinder; there are more brave, out and proud couples in the area (not just in the alternative haven of Utah's Sugarhouse). Even if your coming out experience is not so bad and you can't relate to my experience, finding the stamina it takes to stand against a wall of rejection is hard. As good as things are now in the world, most of us still encounter a whopping dose of rejection in one way or another. I laid down a lot of scar tissue check marks in order to come to grips with it all. Not all of that scar tissue was necessary, but I think it was the way I had to get through it and learn what I needed to. I believe that whatever particular challenges you go through will bring you strengths that will stay with you for the rest of your life.

CHAPTER 7

BULLDYKE BOOGIE MAN

I know the picture in your head: the bull dyke. The picture I once referred to when one would utter the ugly word, LESSSBIAAAANNN.

It was under my bed and in my head when I would turn out my lights—my own personal, teenage, H. E. double-hockey-stick heinous boogieman. My coming-of-age personal lesbonic Chupacabra.

I watched *Poltergeist* once when I was eight. That was blood curdling and I was terrorized for years. I had gone out of my way to sneak a peek at it on TV when I had a babysitter. What a bozo—I had no one to blame but myself, and I dragged my poor, six-year-old brother with me. He had nightmares for a year. I still can't see a clown without twitching and looking over my shoulder for the rest of the day. Sorry, Nick. Yet this was nothing in comparison to *becoming* my worst boogieman.

Yeah, I didn't love wearing dresses, mainly because I couldn't do any cool stuff in dresses. You can't skateboard, bike, jump off things, play kickball, run, or do cherry drops off the high bar in school. They weren't practical, and I did prefer to wear shorts, hands down, on any occasion. I still do. Aren't most girls like that?

No? Hmmmm. I guess I did feel like Halloween when I dolled up like my mom wanted me to. ...

Gulp.

Was I going to become the mannish-hag that I didn't want to be because I had always felt ridiculous when I wore makeup and heels, jewelry and dresses? (There is a certain awkward "dyke in a dress" look that might as well advertise in flashing lights, "Yeah, this one's not gonna like the fellas.") Was it because I felt more like doing the boy things than the girl things about 89 percent of the time? I envied my brothers' lawn-mowing to my cleaning and kitchen chores, and I liked boy clothes better than girl clothes. Then later, it the more pressing fact that I couldn't fall in love with my current boyfriend? (Like, maybe he's just not the right one for me).

"No, dummy," the boogie-dyke would cackle from beneath my bed. "It's because you fell in love with your soccer pal. Wa-ha-ha-ha-aaa!"

She rose from under-the-bed status to my aware consciousness with large, threatening hands on capable, man-repellant hips. She wolfishly directed her gaze sideways, belching at unsuspecting straight girls minding their own disinterested girl business, tapping the ashes of her cigarette onto nice boys and puppies passing by. Perhaps she would give an insulting and inappropriate side-mouthed cat-call while standing with legs unladylike-wide and a jutting jaw, wearing only things deemed "unisex" (which are actually just overwhelmingly masculine without saying Men's on the label).

I don't know about your mind, but that's what came to mine when I heard the word "lesbian" or "lady gay" as a naive, sweet-as-blonde-pie, ignorant and judgy 17-year-old Mormon girl. It was intimidating and ostracizing, because I didn't identify with it, and it was the only kind of ... me? ... I'd seen. I wished I could wear my brother's clothes instead of mine, but didn't want to be overtly boy by doing it. Not necessarily Carharts but Levi's would be nice. Sturdy, tailored, plain, unbreakable, comfortable flannels (stereotype? ching!). I had seen Elton John and some exaggeratedly feminine men on TV. But I didn't even know the name of one gay woman from the media. Knowing only two "out" gay women and having no commonality with or affection for either, I came to the wheel-screeching, horrifyingly straight-train-stopping realization that I liked my teammate and friend *way* too much. More than I cared to. I mean, when her family moved and she stayed with us in order to finish the school year for a few months, I didn't think anything of it. Until I found I was more interested in her than my perfectly handsome and charming, Smiths-loving, alterna-good, hunky, older Mormon boyfriend. Which was just ... weird. Weirder still was that she felt the same for me.

I loved the way she smelled, how she talked, her whole countenance in expression and sleep. My mind lingered on her words. I respected the way she dealt with problems and how she always treated people kindly. She understood and could converse about interesting nuances that were lost on so many others. She "got me" in a wordless way that no one else ever had. I didn't ever even go to the S-E-X scare in my mind. I just wanted her to be closer to me in an unknown, innocent way. Then there were the things she said to me and the way she, too, looked a little longer than was normal—at me.

The motion-detecting light outside the window, which was set off frequently by the many wild things living in our backyard or the wind gusting through the tree, provided mood lighting outside my window well.

By this schizophrenic, unexpected light, I would stare at her and wonder:

What. The heck. Was going on?

This wasn't normal.

Was it?

AAAAAAaaaahhhhh!

Does this happen? Was this happening to me?

No. I'm crazy. Bat-shit creepers.

I should take my multivitamin and eat better. Get more exercise.

It must be her—

I'm a good Mormon girl. I'm normal.

I just want to hold her.

As I wrestled with my feelings in my journal, I would vacillate almost humorously between those first Bambi-eyed, smooshy feelings of confused love—from "I just feel at peace when I'm around her, like there is no better place for me to be" to "No, sin-snacker, You're on the spiritual fast-track to magic-jammy-havin', heavenly planet-making, religious bliss. This cray has come to the wrong door and you'll do nothing to encourage this hateful "thing" creeping up. I'll cut and

47

run, do the right thing, avoid the very impression of anything gay, and never go back. Dresses, long hair, boyfriend—check. You are strong enough to resist any temptation. This especially strong and strange one is no different."

Ouch.

CHAPTER 8

GETTING THE GAY-DAR

I've had many friends, family, and ex-boyfriends ask me sincerely how I knew I was gay, and I think lots of people are genuinely curious, because they ask,

Did my boyfriends just miss the mark?

Was I abused as a child?

Had my boyfriends been smelly, or were they grody?

Did I try enough different types of guys on for size?

You seem girly for a gay; are you *sure*?

Was I in love with my girl friends as a kid?

Did I lack a father figure?

Did I think vaginas were just nicer than penises?

Were my parents gay, or supportive of gays?

Was I exposed to gay porn as an impressionable youth?

Was my father effeminate? Ineffectual?

Did my mother eat too much hormone-infused meat while I was in utero?

Was she distant and uncaring?

Nope. (And yes, these have all been real questions).

I've thought about it and deconstructed it as well as I can. The best way to explain it to someone who is genuinely trying to "get it" is that ...

It's like we're a different species. And we recognize each other somehow.

I can't speak for all gays, because I think lots of people are attracted differently. I'm physically attracted to men; their bodies don't repulse me at all. Objectively, I'm just as objectively attracted to a man's body as a woman's. If my wife Nicole stayed Nicole, but sprouted a man's body, I would still be in love with her and wouldn't care at all that we had another member in the family, as long as it didn't mean extra laundry. As a person who does her fair share of pap-smears and genital exams routinely for work, I have no preference for either set of reproductive parts. At their best, they are tolerable, functional but weird and one sex as icky as the other depending on the day. Point being, the difference isn't just physical. For whatever reason, I just don't get that intrigued, reeled-in feeling with straight women or men. It's reminiscent of how horses don't seem to want to mate with anything other than a horse. Horses can play with cats, enjoy sheep, live with and even love dogs and roosters. But for the bonding part of life, they just don't cross that line. Why would they? If you are straight, did you ever have to sit and really think about who you were attracted to? Probably not very deeply. You just know... as we do.

It seems like the same delineation for me; there's no gray area. And yes, I tested it on curious straight women and men. Among the smaller human pool of gay women we have to choose from, I've found myself only rarely going beyond recognition of "same species" and really, really liking someone. It's exceedingly hard to find that person who is just right on all fronts. But when she has come along, it's a feeling that I want to know more. I get butterflies and can't utter words coherently around them. I blush. I'm more deeply interested and ridiculous—all these things that indicate an inadvertent, undevised psychological and physical response. I want to be closer, to know how she feels, to get to know what's in her head. And if all's good in her head, maybe I'll take the next step.

I used to watch my friends in middle school go through this, and was flabbergasted that my very sane, very cool and collected friends would become puddles of liquid, baby-talking goo with some fumbling guy around. And yes I teased them relentlessly, having not even an inkling of empathy yet for their emotional situation.

I never had that with anyone in the array of different, attractive, amazing guys I dated. It was fine; I could take or leave anything physical; it just didn't matter much. They never got under my skin, and as a result I always felt "cool and aloof" to them, as one put it later. And having dated a few *mostly* straight, Curious George women, it always felt a little off, like I was an "experience" they were having. But it lacked depth and felt more like the fodder that they would use later in life to illustrate their wild youth or open-minded nature to friends when reminiscing.

Even admittedly *unattractive* gay women have that thing ... the vibe, pheromones, I don't know. But that number on the Alfred Kinsey sexuality scale hits right, and a tone is set. No, I don't want every gay girl I see where I get the hit that she's a gay and we're on the same sexuality wavelength. But there's usually a head nod, a longer glance, a recognition of novelty between us—especially when we're floating out in straight land. There's some commonality, and we usually figure each other out.

That's the best way I can find to explain it—for me anyway. I've had male and female gay and transexual friends who differ from me. They have no selectivity in attraction: straight, gay, whatever. If the person is right and they're into them, it's all good. I've had bisexual friends and partners say that the body doesn't matter at all, it's just the person. They have the gay vibe, and they also have the straight thing where you just find yourself attracted to who you like in that gender pool like any straight person. But the gay-dar is a real, sixth-sense thing, and it's how we can spot other LGBTs even when they're so deep in hiding that every gay cue is buried and the opposite "straighter trait" is outwardly broadcasted with convincing fervor.

CHAPTER 9

THE VERY FIRST TIME

I never thought I was the type to blaze a brave trail for an alternative cause or for human rights. I would stand up for many causes—planet, people, or animals, but I didn't want to be "outspoken." I mean, the usual teenage cry for attention, where you pierce something, wear all black, and dye your hair aside, I wanted to be smart and independent—to do well and be bright. To excel but *not* particularly stand out.

Nothing really weird.

I appreciated the weird, befriended and supported the weird, but didn't want to *be* the weird. Visiting the camp vs. living in the camp; these are oh so different. *Especially* regarding something as private as sexuality, made public, by just expressing your whateverness. (The vision of two girls/guys having sex admittedly floats through your head when you find out a couple is gay, right? "No thanks" for this private type.)

Do you do that when you meet your best friend's parents? School teachers' spouses? Not so much. But just out of … logistical curiosity and fascination about what is different, … there it is. The haunting flicker that you then can't let go. You imagine and re-imagine it if you succumb to the curiousity: Is he or she a top or bottom? Did I miss a clue? Is the dominance thing a myth? Do they trade off? But she wears lipstick and dresses. Can a bottom really be that burly? I wish we LGBTs didn't still have to endure this brain quest, but we do.

And we all do it. I admit I do it myself with some people. When the curiosity over logistics passes, and one additionally begins to judge and criticize what's not their business, I hope people will realize what they're doing is unfair and invasive. It's a curiosity because it's different, yes, but should stop there. I don't want to go into your bedroom, why do you have to get into mine?

Back to not wanting to be weird. What I *did* want was to make my parents and people who knew me proud of me, to make God proud of me. I wanted to do amazing things. I wanted a life different than many Mormons girls, in that I knew I wanted to

1. Have a career first
2. Then have a *small* family, as I knew I personally needed to get out and work in the world to be fulfilled.

I didn't want to be embarrassed, and I didn't want to shame my family. I was as horrified as they were when I found out.

Sure, like most gay girls, I was a tomboy. I wasn't attracted to girls physically at all, though. I had no idea I would bend that way, and thought boys were attractive and still do. I wasn't attracted to anyone—boy or girl—with any "umph" behind it until I was 17 (except David Bowie, and that gives no clues to one's tendencies at all). Even then, it didn't seem like *attraction* to my new and closest friend, Jenn, as much as a strange feeling that I connected with and cared for her so much that my heart would burst from my constricted chest.

Our friendship continued to grow until I couldn't breathe or eat or think of anything else. My other friends pegged it and couldn't figure out who I could be whipped over because my I had been with my boyfriend a while and nothing had changed. Man would they have been bowled over to know the crazy truth! Why did I wonder about her all day? What was she was doing, thinking, feeling? I didn't recognize it for what it was, and just kept the best friend gig going in my head, until one day I strangely felt what everyone falling in love feels, ignorant of the occurrence or not. She was upset and crying about something upsetting, whatever teenagers tend to cry about (lame parents or friends, mostly), and I wanted to do anything to fix it. I wanted to take her in my arms and squeeze her, and kiss her forehead to make her feel better.

Innocently I did, until—confused—we both recognized we had been doing that for a long time. We had slept outside on the trampoline because you could bake cookies on the window glass inside the house—it was a scorching hot Utah summer. I still remember the moment when we drew apart, looking at each other, and noticed that something was—off. Both of us sat there looking at each other, and an almost tactile "thought bubble" bobbed above our heads: that gurgled...

I think I know I want to kiss her... when did this change?

Does she feel the same way?

What is this? Why is this happening?

Could this swooney/ lovey feeling be bad?

Is this what all those other girls feel for their guys, and I just thought hey were being dramatic? They weren't being dramatic! They felt like this! I'm so lost. I feel like an idiot.

I am being an idiot.

Now what?

I kissed her that night. Innocently—a slow, trepidatious and soft peck on the lips that meant so much more, because it was a giant leap away from "normal" and was not robotic or "the expected next step," which was precisely how it had felt with my boyfriends. It wasn't the experimental "going through the motions to get a glimpse of what was in store for our adult interactions someday" sometimes typical of common adolescent interaction. It had nothing experimental behind it but a show of what we really felt for each other, in spite of the weirdness, and no drive to go further.

(Where the hell would we go? The plumbing's wrong! Who's in charge? What do you ... and where? How? Whaaaaa? These questions were for much later.)

It was a stumbling trip right into the murky pond of confusion, but also into my first experience of incredible emotional connection.

I had never had those feelings. It wasn't the act. It wasn't a woman's, or girl's, body I wanted. I didn't *not* want my boyfriend's. It was that bond I couldn't explain that caused the attraction. Something else I needed—that something was the feeling that got under my skin and flipped the light switch. It was the feeling that made me want to stay by her side, hold her hand, look into her eyes and make sure she was ok, to try to be the one who would make her happy.

The first forays into physical moving-on were disorienting and uncomfortable, but they nevertheless felt very natural. They were the same feelings that come to most kids who are feeling attraction for the first time that are "normal." We were fast becoming aware that our same gender experience was *not* normal even when it felt that way. So I let the shame in when I didn't have to, and in our inexperience and embarrassment, we fell victim to outside influence.

We had to hide. It tainted the feeling that should have been so elating the first time, and made it hasty, hidey, and halted a good thing.

Even now, thinking of driving to her house, knowing I would stay over (with my parents out of town) and what might happen, my stomach replays it's acrobatics: trapeze figures flipping onto the net of my throat, bounding down to my diaphragm with frustrated, excited flip turns. I felt weak when I smelled her laundry detergent mixed with her innocuous clean lotion on the air as she walked by. I was still so confused about what this feeling was; I wasn't convinced it was wrong. The word gay and the feelings I had didn't match, and they never even occurred to me. One was so gross in my book, yet this incongruous feeling of friendship and love were not at all. It was beautiful. It was so genuine, or it never would have happened. I was the church Seminary president for Gads sake! I was straight as an arrow—jeez, my friends' parents would call me to "check up and get the story" when they were worried about their children. The feelings Jenn and I had for each other had to surmount the overwhelming social taboos it held. Slowly they did.

Needless to say, after a peck on the lips and lingering hugs; holding each other through the night eventually turned into breath-catching touches of the hand or neck or the waist. One of those nights I remember it was dark. We were so close, just holding each other, dozing a little here and there but not wanting to take time with each other for granted by sleeping, so struggling to stay awake, blinking into the darkness. Sometimes we held each other so tightly we would breathe each other's breath. Then I felt her kiss my chin, my cheek. My stomach clenched in the dark. I couldn't breathe. I couldn't think or move as my lips finally met hers, and a kiss that you would give on the head of a child happened for the first time. But I melted to it. I was unable to think of anything or anyone but her. I felt boundless—ridiculous and unprepared—but willing to figure it out. Like the love songs that rolled my eyes back in my head in grossed-out exasperation.

But then the questions came. The need for a label and a judgment. My type-A brain fell to it's reflexive categorizing. What is this?

It was clear, the next step was what, I guess, in retrospect, I had wanted to happen but didn't know I had wanted. A kiss like the cheesy, God-awful movie star kisses we laughed at as kids. Not being able to get close enough. I can't even think what would come after kissing her—even a Mormon girl's imagination wanders to what happens *after* marriage to your man. Not only was this cart going sideways without a clear destination or horse, I was becoming pretty sure the next step in this foray was never going to be sanctioned by the forces that ruled my life. So this cart also had no road.

God, did everyone have to think so hard about all this?

I allowed myself a few more nights of breathing her in, kisses that grew deeper and held on with nowhere to go.

To the *idea* of love.

Logistically, this left nothing but a confused and lingering desire without a map *or* directions, a desire that rushed headlong into lamp posts, tripped off curbs, and bumped into walls with misdirected fits of intention and hesitation.

The penny dropped one night when I was listening to the radio on the way home from the pizza joint, where I worked with my friends and my boyfriend at the time. I heard something on the news about gays and lesbians fighting for rights, blahbity-blah. Then it struck me out of the blue. I realized the feeling I felt for Jenn equaled the definition of "gay." How different was I from the topic on the radio? Is that what this feeling was? The question froze me stock-still. I had to pull my car over, nose crinkled as if engulfed in a bog of stinky cheese, in disgust at the dawning realization of my course. It had a name, and it was gay.

Gayness was happening.

The word lesbian was creepy. To me. I hated it and couldn't believe it. I started to think and feel with two decidedly different parts—one tainted brain and one open heart. How could love for a person, where no harm is being done, be so wrong? I had never felt so right in my life, as by her side.

And vice versa: the good and the bad. The cold, firm hand of the gay label crept in (echo, ... echo, ... echo ...) and, despite the warmth of my feelings for her, I was so ensconsed in a judging mentality, that it cast a chilled and deforming shadow on her. On us. It was wrong. "Sinful and disgusting."

Then why didn't it feel that way?

I shuddered and was physically sick (TMI, sorry).

I was crestfallen, and she was unsuspecting of my realization.

I finished it the very next time I saw her.

I stayed away and coldly asked her to do the same. I didn't even entertain the idea of anything with another girl until years later when of course this "strange anomaly of attraction" of course resurfaced in a different situation with a different person. I lost Jenn as a friend and first love in a horribly sad way because of the darkness cast by the church's harsh influence.

CHAPTER 10

OH YEAH? I BROKE UP WITH YOU FIRST!

Granted, by the time I was a late teen I had some long-standing questions about the doctrine of the church that hadn't been answered to my satisfaction. I had my gaping doubts in places. But in the back of my washed, washed brain, I thought I would eventually get through it by letting the aforementioned "spirit of the law" run things in the end (that is, trusting in the spirit to fill in the stuff I don't understand or consciously agree with in time). This is a common recommendation by the church when we don't understand, or question aspects of doctrine or practice. Questioning some things that flat out don't make sense to me doesn't earn me challenges of creepy feelings and gay, warped rollercoasters, does it? Did it?

What. The. Frock.

So ... I'd get rid of my first real crush—my first inkling of love in a girl named Jenn. A Mormon girl who was incredibly genuine, sweet, attractive, smart, cool and kind, and equally confused. I'd kick her to the curb for the church. She could take her incognito gay voodoo elsewhere—I wasn't drinking that Eve juice, Batman! Then, I'd lie in wait for it to make sense in time, because an answer would come eventually, right?

And that's what I did. To solve at once the problem of unexpected and unwanted attraction.

Right.

What an asshole. (Admittedly not an ok Mo swear, but in this case wholly appropriate and unfit for substitution.)

I still look back and realize that because of my fear and conditioning, I made a scary thing for both of us so much worse for her. She didn't quit so easily; to her credit she was a much better friend than I was, and more true to her self. She had tried to keep in touch. She wanted to be friends, to normalize it, play it off, and was willing to deny the reality of our relationship as I wanted to. Even go on double dates with our boyfriends...

I couldn't imagine being around her and not being *with* her! I knew that would feel too twistedly fake to ever make it work and that just acting like her friend was a sure way to be found out in time. I could envision double dating while having to feign interest in my boyfriend all night, laughing at jokes on cue and acting interested. All while keenly watching her every move and feigning that I *wasn't* thinking that everything she said was funny and fascinating. Until we would accidentally brush hands on our napkins at the same time, and Poof! I would burst into flames of blushing fluster. Everyone would see that, and our cover would be blown! The horror unleashed! Great idea.

Jenn didn't deserve my dismissive cold shoulder, however, and I've always regretted my lack of authenticity with her. I just hadn't matured enough to deal with this scary and emotional situation gracefully yet, so I freaked. It's like when your cat brings you a partly dead mouse and plops it on your lap—a thoughtful, hard-won show of love and affection: "Thank you for feeding me, housing me, and doing that scratchy ear thing you do." Instead of thanking him, you trip out and fling the twitching, bloody mouse from your lap before you can muster up the sense to think of another's feelings. It's a fight or flight reaction. *"Get to safety, and run away. Also, scream."*

I couldn't reconcile my "should's" and "rules" to depart from the restrictive church doctrine on that topic for anything, even her. The only thing I could do was get away from her at all costs. Being friends was even too close—Pandora's dirty Box in my circle of friends was a recipe for disaster. I would give in and be close to her again if I were around her for any period of time. It sounds extreme, but it took all the strength I had to stay away from the first glimpse of love I had in a life where I didn't usually feel very neat or loved for who I was. Someone who saw the real me and *loved* me, and who I loved in return. I had never been that close to anyone before. I was weak for her: would do *almost* anything for her. Her only competition was God. To me, Jenn felt like the reason humans are on this planet, and felt consistent with the spirit of the God I loved. But the rules of the church said otherwise, so I decided not to risk acting on my feelings for her and losing my spiritual identity.

Discrimination and hate took over. Hate of something I didn't even understand—gayness. It was just an idea, a word, to me. But it overcame a feeling as strong as first love, and it won.

Religion won over spirituality, and fear overcame understanding. I was in no way ready to put myself in the camp of the mannish lady gays I'd seen. No. *Heck* no.

Even though Jenn *wasn't* mannish, and who cares if she was. She was really funny and pretty. She handled things with class. She was well respected and such a cool, intelligent person. I had many difficult, shame-bearing, tooth-gnashy years to travel before I would have an equivalent presence.

CHAPTER 11

THE BOOKS

Many years later, I read through my coming out journal with pained, fake laughter at my desperate attempts to hide myself as I "found" myself. I had disguised Jenn as *Jason*, and rigged the journal with pronouns, making she's into he's. It's very confusing to read; alluding to homosexual struggles, then writing of my outlawed longing for *Shawn*, wishing I could change the love I felt, apply the same feelings to another person, and feel less shameful for it. I had diaphanous visions of loved ones uncovering my journal of confessions after an unexpected and deadly accident, leafing through my dirty laundry not expecting to find such icky secrets. I couldn't stand the idea of being found out—even after I was dead. The retrospective embarrassment would have been unbearable. Sue became good old *Shawn*. And I do mean old. It's one thing to sin with your missionary a little bit, when he's going away for two, celibate years. A natural, opposite-sex, age appropriate, heavy-petting scenario is deliciously scandalous and interestingly naughty but not disgusting and stomach-turning gnarly in church land. It's an entirely different and nose-scrunching, gag-inducing sin to jump into the dark, dirty-bird, twisted waters of same-sex messing around. Even *considering* it was just.

Wow. Seriously, ... Ew.

Such a game changer. You can't wipe that brain slate clean.

Once the weight of curiosity and determination overcame the embarrassment of getting caught investigating the gays, I sought to do what I always do. I put my nose in a book and retreated for a while to think and marinate in what I read. To figure life out by taking in the sage words of someone who has done this before.

I had a whole story (sketched out on a paper to read if I got too nervous to remember it), that I was going to spew to the person who worked at the information desk if they gave me a funny look about my topic of "research": homosexuality and Mormonism. It consisted of complete lies sandwiched in stories of "thesis research." I was doing studies of monkeys or fruit flies or some such total bullshirt that had to do with me being a biology major (transcript available for whipping out if eyebrows queried my long tale ... as if). The poor guy at the desk tolerated about two sentences more of my spiel than he cared to hear, before directing me irritably to the literature that was available on the topic.

One book. *The* book.

It was bright blue. It looked brand, spankin' new. It's shiny cover had slippery, almost reflective, mocking canary yellow letters sprawling "Born That Way?" in cursive across it. Why did it have to be so flashy? Talk about grandiose! Just shut it and say what you need to without embarrassing me alreadyyyyyyy (in snitty, teenage voice).

It had never been touched by any other queirdo before, I was sure. Except by the guy who received it hot off the press from the truck and had to place it on the shelf, looking both ways and puffing his chest with a disconnected air and a masculinized general disposition after depositing it away from him onto the shelf. There the book would stand, collecting lonely dust for years, until a strange event made a Mormon like me feel like a freak of nature enough to go hunting for answers in it.

Then there was me. I slunk along with wide and panicky eyes, hanging so much on the words within this text—*my hooOOOoooly future*, I thought. I tried hard to appear to be browsing the shelves casually, like ... sure ... yawn ... whatever, while my heart flooded my embarrassed cheeks. After finding the glitzy "look at me, I'm a gay," drag-queen of a book, I reflexively slipped off the gleaming cover so that I could slink outta there incognito to check it out while making efforts to breathe normally and stop fidgeting like a nail biter with Tabasco fingers. Could I employ its wisdom to fix me and make it all better? I was *only* searching for the answers to the universe, this creepy, homo universe that was threatening my respectable life as I knew it and claiming me against my will. No pressure, right?

The book became my paper vampire, lurking patiently in the dark coffin of my backpack by day, only to be surreptitiously brought out at night under my sheet where I would feed hungrily by flashlight so as to remain undiscovered as a gay content reader to my dorm roomies. (I was randomly matched with five small-town Mormon cheerleaders from Tremonton, UT: pronounced *tree-mon-eeeeen*. It was them and then me, a small-haired, granola-hipster dufus. I was lost in a sea of giant hair. To my utter surprise I came to love those girls. They were not shy about how alien I was to them, and they fully embraced me in all my plain otherness). Unaware of my dark struggles, they dragged me into their little group of friends, and I did not want to lose the "different but fun" vibe I had, to the "terminally different" vibe I would adopt if I admitted to being gay.

Anyway, petrified of being found out, I would read through the night in my ridiculous, college dorm "fort" of covers after everyone else finally went to sleep. After recognizing that the author and I had indeed encountered the same garish sexuality issues, I felt a camaraderie that was strangely comforting after having felt so alone for so long. I read on and realized that this author was not the well-balanced authority on the broad topic that I needed. He had his lone experience, did the best he could with his life, and shared it kindly in his pages. But it wasn't the investigation of options from a Mormon view that I wanted. I wanted the full exposé, including but not limited to the following questions:

How did we get like this?

Is it my fault?

I'm not allowing this behavior, why isn't it changing my feelings?

How is it possible to live this way if we can't fix it?

Is it genetic, and can I extract the gene and put in down the garbage disposal?

How many of us are there?

Where are they, and are they allowed out in the day time?

Is Santa Claus real?

My unfair expectations aside, the author was narrowly informed by the church. The book only looked at one side of the issue, and came to conclusions based on fear: follow the rules without first asking the impetus, logic, and accuracy behind the rules. I read and re-read this one and only book available to me, and as I digested the fact that the book was a call to denial, or "overcoming" what I knew couldn't be changed, I wept like a little girl. I had hoped for a magic fix in this book. I longed for inspiration I could trust. Even if I reached the conclusion that I had to just live life alone, or live a hetero-imposter life, I wanted an enlightened advisor to give me trustworthy reasons to do so. I may have swallowed it if *Born That Way?* had presented me with a well-studied, emotionally and intellectually balanced landscape. I wanted to be pulled by convincing stories on both sides of the coin, given compelling evidence. I wanted to understand the history of this thing before I could make an educated decision and be at peace with it.

I ached for the spine to rise up, to answer my cry for help. But the book only left me wanting and so very ... disappointed. I wanted anything but the perpetuation of shame and rules it offered.

At that age, who listens to the voice inside that says: "Relax already, you're fine the way you were made?"

Ok, well, some people do.

I didn't. I told myself I was just rationalizing in order to get what I wanted, which was morally weak. It was a never-ending mind game that disabled me in the "thinking for myself" department. It was new to me to have to generate original thought outside this religion's box. If I thought, "Hmmm, I'm God's child, and He made me this way, so I *must* be fine the way I'm made" or "How could a feeling like love be *bad*? ... maybe they don't know the whole story," I would soon circle back to thinking I was just manipulating my thinking to let me get what I wanted. And then I would circle back to, "I didn't just suddenly become evil! This makes no sense!".

The weak answer: (in stony surfer dude voice) "I know, right? Seriously. Nothin wrong with you, man!"

The responsible answer: (hands on hips, tapping foot lady with a stern, tight bun and brown skirt suit) "Well somehow I must have let something evil slip in, and every time I question it, I'm delaying accountability, keeping the approved and proper spirit with me, and postponing forward progress."

La-de-dah, my million thoughts were continually dissected and then Frankenstein- patched back to what I hoped was presentable. My rationally trained religious mind would speak up and say that it was the voice of doubt sneaking in. I couldn't entertain the devil's "normalizing" of ungodly thoughts, and this was how he got in. Little thoughts, doubts, questioning what I had been told. Leaving the teachings of the church is a catch-22. You can't do it without threat of eternal demerit! Unfortunately, I was still in the practice of looking to *others* to teach me things-who am I to decide matters of importance? I'm just some little blonde queer, sloshing around in a big wave pool of uncertainty. Who am I to question the rules of time-tried religion or elders with sage, biblical words and long beards? Who am I to receive my own divine guidance and trust my own feelings and intuition on a very salient matter?

I began staying out of the dorm then, in search of a hole to crawl into. I would wander around at all hours of the night, not caring about the foolishness of that behavior. I can't claim naiveté, in all honesty. In retrospect it was the beginnings of what developed into intentionally reckless behavior. I was daring something to happen. Daring something to wipe this life clean and swiftly gondola lift me up to the next life without having to suffer through this one any more. This would evolve into finding alternative ways to get around suffering. Alcohol helped, and I initially forced its use to see what the fuss was about and to show that I was out of the church, even though beer tasted like a double-dog dare of grossness. It was quite clear with a cigarette in hand and a beer in the other that you aint in Mo' camp no more. And with the small, segregated nature of Utah communities at the time, a quick, easy, non-Mormon group of compatriots was not hard to find.

I got a job at a cool pizza hang-out bar with live music and found a cool crowd of people in my small college town. Some gay girls figured me out and came down to play pool until I was off work, with the intent to recruit me for rugby. I laughed, halfheartedly said I was straight, and that I would like for all my bones to remain unbroken. The captain of the team was named D (for Daliah). She looked right at me, called bologna, and told me to be at the pitch at 3.

It just so happened I didn't have to work or study that day, so I "stumbled" upon them sheepishly. After the second practice, I had signed on to get my booty kicked publicly for Utah State University by women larger and in-charger than myself. I was once dragged more than a quarter of the way down the pitch by a Tongan woman who—I'm pretty sure—didn't even know I was hanging at her ankles trying to take her down. It was so much fun. It was the start of greater exposure: lots of gay girls squeezed into rugby jerseys, packed-car road-trips, drink-ups, fake IDs, and good times being more comfortable with who I was.

So there I was, a junior in college, and truly done with the church. I knew then I wouldn't ever go back to it, and, as in the end of any relationship, I started to see all the obvious flaws in it, and the doubts I had all along.

"Oh yeah? I shoulda dumped you when … !"

What took me so long? I felt so silly—or two faced—for going along with the church when I disagreed with so much of it for so long. It's just that … the culture, and the members, have such a sweet kindness. It's easy to overlook the doctrine's impasses. I was a typical oldest child—a pleaser who didn't want to drop a sad bomb.

In all honesty, it was a spiritual relief. Pushing back the doubts I had even before this gay thing threatened had become full-time mental exercise. Like a niggling idea that will not be quelled, a canker on the tip of your tongue you just can't stop flicking against your tooth like a lizard with OCD. "Why do only Mormons go to the

Celestial Kingdom? What happens in the afterlife to all the other people who were on this planet before the church was formed and they could become members?" This one just wouldn't sit right, no matter how much faith shmere I applied. I would have left the church eventually; it just would have taken me a bit longer.

So what did I do then? What any rebelling, self-respecting, "whole life repressed but no more as of today," newly ex-Mormon would do. I walked to the 7-11 and bought cigarettes. It was a Friday. I smoked two in a row, anticipating the famous tingle, but instead I just hurled. There happened to be a rugby party that night, which I attended with a clear agenda. I grabbed my first beer and attempted to acquire a taste for the stuff in the span of one evening. After 3 drinks I was a goner, and I proceeded to make out with a couple accommodating ladies happy to help me on my curious, reactionary way. I danced on a table. I played poker with facecards (another strange Mormon no-no).

I woke up on Saturday morning feeling like a forest animal had stored its feces in my mouth for the winter. I was in someone's cabin in the middle of—well, I wasn't at all sure where I was or what had happened the night before. I remember being scared and regretting how this was going down. Then, dancing on a table. This was not as I imagined it would be. Luckily my new friends were real friends and took care of me, and everyone took great pleasure in reliving my wild night for me over my attempt at breakfast. Yes, it's fun to see a prude let go for the first time, doing things that are hilariously out of character. But I felt disembodied, directionless, and so frickin hungover I wanted to take a dirt nap. Why did people like this partying business?

I thought I would just have to practice.

Perhaps I needed to continue to apply a little of the "all things in moderation" law from the Word of Wisdom. It turns out I would need to work on this for years to come. I started investigating alternative ways to get around the anger and discomfort of the gay fallout. Alcohol became a pee–flavored, amnesia-inducing friend and was a swell break from real life dealings, that would eventually present too heavily as a coping skill in my life, requiring heavy pruning and understanding of what I was STILL trying to get out of feeling.

CHAPTER 12

TESTING THE WATERS

Before I could really jump in to being ok with being who I felt like I was naturally, I had some more introspection and convincing of myself to do. Some more gnashing of teeth and self-flaggelation, really.

In my years of studying the LDS doctrine, I got the clear message that if you have the challenge of being gay in this life, you just need to fight through it. Abstain from any expressions of *physical* love, or even nurturing an abnormal *emotional* love, despite what you feel. The church recognizes that there are many who have this "tendency," but the stance continues to be that those afflicted need to "tough it out" so their slates are clean when they die. This is the only way to get the prize of being in the presence of God after the test of this life is over. After going through a year of anti-gay therapy, I considered staying with my boyfriend thinking "Wow, isn't that an uber crappy and unfair thing to do to a nice guy? Marry him and not really *love* love him? Tolerate him, really, as a friend or a pal?

That just seemed rude.

The alternative idea of living my life alone—without sharing love with someone—was also intolerable. Human beings are not put on this planet to live without love; it's not natural for us. We are of God, and God *is* love. Arguably the most important lesson to learn in this life is how to love unconditionally. Isn't making an exception for gender conditional? I know without question that God would not ask me, or other anomalies to the heterosexual mold, to live a lie or live without love.

The church and I were calling it quits, and I was interested in moving on. The LDS doctrine just didn't make sense to me anymore, especially after traveling and seeing more of the "unsaved" world. This is what brought it home: There are so many variables in how we as human beings look. In how we speak. In how we function, express our talents and repress our fears.

In how we work, love, drive, dance, worship, walk, write, sneeze, carry our children, celebrate and mourn.

Why is it not yet an accepted fact that the variability we see *everywhere* in life should also naturally apply to attraction and gender identification, and love?

It took me a long time to embrace this concept of loving everyone in their difference, without judgement. Most importantly, myself! I had to ditch the profound sense of shame and guilt for being born an outsider- or an apostate as we are now called. Some days I realize I still have a lot of work to do to meet this goal. On more balanced days I realize that difficulty in knowing and embracing who we are is part of the human condition and not just an LGBT issue.

Most of us are amazing, emotional, and spiritual beings, meant to realize our full potential on Earth. But it's a lifelong journey. Some journeys are made with perforated tires, bloody knees, looking like trauma victims as they drag their zombie remains across the finish line. Some lucky busters seem to glide through puffy clouds with candy canes and fairy wings, with very few jostling bumps in the road of life (don't you want to punch them?).

As humans beings in this world, we're meant to learn how to show love and compassion to each other. LGBTs don't need to change to be worthy of that love, even if we could! Let's stop perpetuating a culture where the first instinct of gays and those around them wish for that. Let's stop dating and breaking the hearts of nice straight people by being dishonest. The only way in which we really differ from heterosexuals is breeding, really. The gay sides of each gender sometimes lean toward the traits of the other gender. What is the harm of falling outside of the predictable box? There is no threat in these things. We no longer need to repopulate the world, people. Seven billion on a shrinking Earth: I think we're good. We've established our species. So what's the harm in two men or women getting hitched? Or in someone switching teams to feel authentic to their true self?

I tried my darndest (my dad's favorite Mo swear- so cute) to change myself in anti-gay therapy. Right up to the moment when they recommended shock therapy treatment. Having read about conversion therapy, it sounds just as horrible as shock treatment with the claim of being able to cure homosexuality. The theory of shock therapy is that you can "change" your response to people or things by pairing painful stimuli with images or associations you previously found pleasurable, but no longer want to. Like cake, or alcohol, or kissing girls. Zap! But I'm here to tell you, you can suppress your sexuality, *but you cannot change* that part of you that loves whom it will. If you stuff it somewhere, it will pop up somewhere else like a maddening game of Whack a Mole, where you know you lose, because the game cheats. You never win. Ever. Your sexuality is undaunted by your attempts at shaping it. It perseveres as its own entity. I'm not saying you can't control what you do, but if you don't give your love an outlet, it finds another that may not be as palatable. Anyone who abides severe sexual repression is riding a rodeo bull with a blinding blanket, just hoping to influence the charge of the beast. Attraction and sexuality are more than just sex. It's a matter of love in all it's expressions and when denied, it just rides *you* into subliminal ... then eventually not so subliminal ... frustration or, at worst, despair or violence.

CHAPTER 13

TAKING THE PLUNGE

So I guess I'll pick up a few years after my first gay glimmer with Jenn in high school. Of course (shocked gasp!) I had another attraction "anomaly" like the one that had afflicted me as a precariously vulnerable youth, a.k.a. a girl crush. When I was 19, I met the third openly gay woman I had ever known. She was so mal-aligned with me as a person, my goals, beliefs, core interests, generational age, etc. I couldn't imagine a less likely match. But she had that "thing" I couldn't explain, and yet was so strangely attracted to, and she owned it. She had a horrible Susan Powter haircut and practically wore a tool belt, for the love of all that's holy.

Her name was Jordan (for the purposes of this book). She was just *out there* to everyone, and she was unapologetic about being a mega gay-wad. I was scared and fascinated all at once. It felt exactly like driving by a horrible car accident and not being able to turn your head away despite people honking behind you. That hetero-unreproducible, connection and emotional pull was the beginning of my final slide into the murky gay pool of mysterious weird awesomeness. Meeting her was the occasion for me to peel away from the entrenched religious belief that I must follow all of the church's constructs or live the rest of eternity in a fiery hell of regret and self-loathing. It was the end of my self-reprimand to stay strong for just one, measly lifetime in order to have my eternal bounty, like, squared away for good.

Well, I processed all of these ideas after formally failing a true effort at anti-gay therapy, and my instincts coalesced. I was officially done. In the weeks to come, I worked doing odd jobs one night with the mannish lady-gay I couldn't stop being attracted to. She told me, as I redundantly rolled paint onto the lofty ceiling of our worksite, that she got a gay vibe from me when we first met. My heart skipped a beat, and I slopped paint onto our employers' fancy carpet when I defensively swiped my arms to my sides. I feigned horror and indignation. I queried why the heck she would say that, and asked the oh-so-frequent question: "What is gay-dar? How can you tell? How can you be sure? Well, yours is broken" I couldn't stop asking her questions, pressing for some solid information or clue at connection, while trying to take on an air of mild amusement and disinterest. Instead, I was nervous and acting like my stupid friends did around their crushes in junior high. I could barely talk—I stammered. I eventually got close to her when I playfully flicked her stinky cigarette out of her fingers on her smoke break, and she pulled me in close. I had to close my eyes; I couldn't breathe. Plus, cigarette smoke, ew. She kissed me patiently, expertly, knowing what a confusing struggle I must have been going through. Even before I drew away from her, I knew I would never go back. Everything about it felt right, and she wasn't even a Jenn to me. She was kind and patient, but 40 to my 19, and going through a big break-up. We recognized our limited relationship for what it was, and she was great in the job of prying my nascent gay out of hiding.

I tried one more time to date a hippie artist guy I liked SO much, just in case there could be any possibility.

It ended badly. I hurt him deeply and still feel guilt for that last selfish stab at denial. He didn't deserve it. I knew beyond a doubt. But thick heads be thick, and I am nothing if not thorough. Like a "stubborn ole donkey", as my grandfather would lovingly point out.

After that I left my college town, moved back to Salt Lake City, and dated women. I came out to my family later that year and got my first real girlfriend for two years. Another unlikely match, but I did love her, and I started to see for myself and truly believe that this was the authentic, higher me. It felt spot on, and I was completely satisfied just being true to my nature, even though I was not yet so spot on about my choice in partners. I had many years of honing work to do on that one, but the hard part was done and was all worth it.

CHAPTER 14

MOM. OUT WITH IT ALREADY.

Back in the day, a typical introductory conversation among gays where I was from began with, "How is your family with it/do they know?" "How did you come out?" followed inevitably, assuming the friend wasn't still dwelling in the closet with old sweaters and moth balls. Coming out is almost universally a family crisis with vigor to rival Spanish soap operas. It's reliably juicy conversation.

Unlike Jesse's magnificent outing addressed later, I exited the closet in a Toyota Camry: first to my mom, in our "fancy," new-to-us, light blue, used version after we parked it in the garage. It had taken me so long to work up the courage to get to this point; I couldn't believe it was real. My sweaty palms tingled with anxiety, and I marveled as the words birthed themselves from penumbra into the pastel Camry darkness.

Was I *sure* I needed my family to know about the real me? Couldn't I continue the façade for a lifetime and spare myself this humiliating exertion? I fumbled until the words lifted from my mouth like ghostly regrets. After dancing around the topic for seven bumpy miles home, I unfurled the molasses words, "I'mmmmmmm ggaaaaaaaaayyyyyy." No take-backs now, no do-overs or claims of "eh-heh, I was just kidding back there when I said that." I had practiced those words so many times, and yet only the bare, fear-baked bones of my speech made it to the air. I had such deep fear of what she would do. We had our differences—huge differences—but she loved me and had

74

always done as well as she could with her tomboy teen. Could she get through this?

I expected shock, some level of surprise, or even a raised eyebrow and a controlled throat catch. Perhaps some dramatic vomit; my mom did have flair. But to my mixed relief and dismay, what crossed my mother's face was a knowing, slightly surrendered look. A kind visage revealing the resigned recognition of what she had known for many years. She even had a little head nodding, with the slightly pursed, turned up smile that hinted to me: Yeah. You know we've suspected this since you were seven and insisted on wearing basketball shorts and striped, knee-high tube socks while dribbling a basketball everywhere you went. Yeah, It crossed our minds.

I'm not so much in lady-man gender mystery camp. Maybe a bit on the boyish side, but feminine enough that it doesn't hit you over the head. Once the suggestion has been made, *then* you can see the gayish. It's like the *Where's Waldo?* books after you expertly spot him on the page and thereafter cannot remember how it was you couldn't see him from the start.

In light of the little gay-wad giveaways of my personality that don't necessarily scream but rather croak between a whisper and a low and drag queenie "heeeeeyyyy," in retrospect, I think many people knew before I did. I was too clueless to even *try* to hide the few but glaring neon signs. I turned down a cute, popular prom date to go to a soccer game. I admit to a mullet and short-cropped hair (but only in the 80s when everyone was doing it). It took an act of Congress for my mom to get me into a dress and make-up, when all I wanted to do was hike the beautiful mountains of Utah by myself and listen to my moody alternative music (instead of the musical voices of hot guys on the phone). My aunt Tammy said she knew when I brought a book with me on a date in high school. What? That's weird? I might get bored....

I will forever thank my mom for what came next for two reasons:

1. I knew she would love me anyway, no matter what. And for a little while, she even questioned how her church could reject

her child who hadn't *done* anything to be this way. I can count on one hand how many of my ex-Mormoning friends got that response right off the bat. Mom, you are the best kind of parent, and you should know this. So in return I will tell your gruff and grumpy new husband about himself after I've had two glasses of wine, because he doesn't treat you as well as you deserve. You're welcome. I mean, I'm sorry.

2. She gifted me with one of the funniest coming-out stories of all time. Now my mom was sweet, as I've said. But she is not naive, and she had "lived a little" before getting hitched to my dad in the big Salt Lake City. She was from a small town in Washington, and it was a big move to start her life anew. In her college days she had sowed some wild oats. She knew what was out there, at least more than I did at my innocent age. She had been with an "older man" at that time and- don't ask me how I knew this- but had tried "the weed" (please see air quote fingers), as well as alcohol at one point. It felt so scandalous and intriguing when I found this out about her: like she had shiny secrets and other lives lived with secret trapdoors and hushed heat. She had repented of course and gone back to "the fold," with what I perceived as contrite regret for short-lived bad behavior, to assume again the sweet, Mormon woman yoke. She mostly kept the part, and is a genuinely kind sort of Mormon. But there's something smart and knowing, something kind of sassy about my mom that I love. And here it is:

After I blurt out the non-shocking "I'm gay" utterance, and she nods her head telling me it's not entirely a shock, we continue to talk about how I know. "Do you have a ... girlfriend?" she asks (nose scrunched as if I'm waving dirty gym socks beneath her nose). "Have you talked to... anyone?"

"Yes," I said, "I've talked to a counselor once a week in anti-gay therapy for a year." To this her eyes showed tear-filled sympathy, and she patted my shoulder lovingly. "Haven't you had boyfriends you've liked?" Yes, from gorgeous college football player to artistic and soulful hippy. "Well," she said slowly and in a conspiratorial tone, "I may be in trouble for saying this, ... but (with sly grin on her abashed face) "why don't you just try it? Maybe just do it once?" (Mom then corrected herself, mumbling the first time isn't always so great, maybe give it a few—then again catching herself and pursed her lips as if to stop the talking from coming out of her.) Then she stammered, "I mean if you think you're sure, and you're going to go with ... the gay ... thing anyway. What do you have to lose?"

Blink. The garage door light timed out, and we sat alone in the dark.

I looked toward her side-lit face, which was a blur of so many emotions, I couldn't fish any one out, and asked, "Uh, mom? Are you saying I should go have pre-marital sex with a guy as an experiment to prove gayness?"

We couldn't stand it anymore; we burst out laughing. I snorted out loud. Mom shook so hard with her hands over her eyes, I thought she was having a seizure. All the tension I had created by trying to break some serious news to her that she had already known was broken. I'm not saying she was cool with it. She was disappointed and fearful of my now unsure future. HIV/AIDS came to her mind, and she feared for my safety. She feared I wouldn't have children of my own. She feared I wouldn't have a long-term, dependable partner. Without a safe and loving family to go to in the future—the most treasured Mormon value (families can be together forever)—how could I truly lead a fulfilled life?

I couldn't convince Mom it would be okay, because I didn't know! I had no role models. There was no public Ellen DeGeneres to soften the blow of what shot into people's heads when hearing the "L" word. I thought, *I may want kids one day*, but I was a career-path girl all the way, and none of those things were entering my driven mind at that stage. Most of my straight friends at the time would be marrying within four years or so, as was the general standard in Utah. I couldn't reassure Mom about anything other than that I would always do my best to be true to myself and how I was raised. My mom trusted that and was a devoted parent through the hard times, embarrassing times, friends-with-green-mohawks-for-Thanksgiving-dinner times.

I have always known how lucky I am to have her, and I hope she knows I'll never forget.

Chapter 15

Pre-Alien Abduction Dad

My parents divorced when I was eleven. After that, my father began referring to me as a cat: While the other three kids were puppies clambering for his lap when they saw him every other weekend, I was more aloof. It was a well-known fact that my father didn't like cats. He only half-jokingly swerved the car toward them when he saw them on the street. I knew he cared deeply for me—he had always been very loving. He just didn't like this new ... phase.

I was a predictably awkward pre-teen with a tomboy twist and would be sitting on no one's lap anymore in any circumstance, thank you very much.

On top of this, I felt the sky falling when I was around Dad, because he was still raw with anger and emotion at my mom for ruining their eternal marriage. He couldn't always hold his tongue around us kids on his weekends. He didn't ever badmouth her intentionally; it would just gurgle out of him, painfully, like the airy burps from the depths of a gloppy mud bog. My heart wrung for him—I had identified with him throughout my childhood, and we had been thick as thieves to that point. He was devastated by the divorce. I hated seeing him that way, and to cope I put some distance between me and that view until I hoped he could resurface and be himself again. Moreover, I felt defensive of my mother when the gurgling started. Finally, for the cherry on this sad-shit sundae, I felt some responsibility in the failure of their marriage. If I had

79

been more helpful, taken more stress from my parents by helping even more around the house (as he had previously suggested)—keeping the other kids in line—I thought I could have turned things around.

So, apparently, I donned the unsavory armor of a finicky feline, much to his dismay. I was also working very hard on making some friends at the umpteenth school I was going to, having moved almost every two years up to that point, and that required more investment than two weekends a month afforded.

I went with him on his weekends less frequently, and enjoyed his despairing company less when I did go. Distance slowly took shape in the spaces where we used to play catch, laugh, and have tickle wars until we cried "uncle." He thought I was siding with my mom, but I was just trying to stay under the catastrophe radar and have some semblance of normal-kid life. And to be honest, as the responsible oldest girl of divorced working parents, I liked having some time off from the other puppies. They broke my stuff, elbowed, jerked and rustled me when I just wanted to be in my own, self-absorbed, pre-teen haven of gloomy, deep music, weird art, transporting books, and brooding thoughts. I don't know how anyone could resist me, really. Let's just assume I was no ray of golden sunshine, and he likely didn't enjoy my company much at that point either.

Consequently, I thought it would leave less hair to rip under the band-aid, making it easier to handle when he turned the cold shoulder with my coming out years later. I knew he wouldn't be cool with it in any way, shape, or form. When he found out from my siblings before I could tell him myself, he proved this by sending *boxes* of anti-gay literature to my dorm room (which was received by the very straight, very unknowing, small-town cheerleaders, much to my complete humiliation). There were multiple, long coercive phone calls without understanding or real emotional connection; he said nothing directly to me as his daughter, just a prepared sermon for the damned. The blow hurt worse than I thought it would, despite our emotional drift prior to the unveiling. In retrospect he was doing what he thought was his responsibility: trying to save my soul by bringing me back to the flock in his own way. And admittedly, he was trying to save some face as well. I was an embarrassment to him—a badge of his failure in spite of his fatherly righteousness. He would reiterate church doctrine over and over again, in case I had missed the gist of all I had learned in my previous 18 years of Seminary (school-based study of LDS doctrine that you can take as a Junior high/high school elective). I had taken this class every morning at the crack o' dawn before regular school started, as well as;

Sunday School groups,

Visiting teachers who came to our house weekly, per the standard,

Three hour church sessions every Sunday of my life, and

Mutual Classes(an age- and sex-specific church gathering) every midweek with church-based service projects in between.

Plenty of time to pick up on the doctrine, if you ask me.

Dad's condemnation and rejection hurt me deeply, and his dogged persistence blew my mind. Did he really think I just had a bad idea and abandoned my previous ideals on a whim with no thought to consequence or history? It seared into my inferior-feeling, fragile, striving gay heart that this was what I would encounter from everyone for the rest of my life. If my own dad would so readily be this way, why would anyone else be kinder?

Dad's cold shoulders, and my own disappointment in my stunted plan for my life, poured gasoline on the flame of fear that was already rising and helped to ignite more self-loathing and uncharacteristic behavior. I didn't feel like a loved "child of God." I felt like a faux pas. I hadn't even *acted* on feelings of being gay yet!

Well, here I go then!

Within a few days of my final decision and the family fallout, I submersed myself, without overt grace, into non-Mormon life and habits. In my opinion, a kid feeling less inflamed by rejection by loved ones would act less drastically. People coming of age will experiment and figure things out regardless, but perhaps they should do it with less fury and more moderation than I did.

I know now and I knew then, that no one could "make" me do something, or feel a certain way unless I allowed it to. My actions were my own choice and can't be blamed on anyone else; I don't blame my father or friends for my reckless behavior. I say it for the parents of a gay kid who may read this. Even if you *do* feel ashamed of your daughter or son now, if you care about them and want to keep them safe through a potentially unstable and scary transition, let them know you love them and keep them close. Talk to them! It doesn't need to be (and shouldn't be) about what's happening in their love or sex life. Talk to them about Grandma and the weather and ... your broken muffler. Whom they're dating if you're daring and can listen without wincing (it means a lot if you ask, but says the wrong thing if you ask but can't stand to hear the answer. Feel free to ease in slowly). Nothing you do or say will influence your child to behave with less care for his or her well being than your rejection and shame in them. Whether or not kids *want* to care about what their parents think of them, they do. And if they lose your respect just by being how they were made, then what do they have to lose by acting out?

The most secure and stable gay friends I had during this tumultuous time were the ones whose parents continued to love and support them. Not necessarily waving pom-poms and bellowing gay cheers to the heavens, but loving unconditionally. These people knew that their choices still mattered because they weren't already condemned. I can't say that all gay kids that had love coming from home behaved safely, either. The point is, the reaction of loved ones *matters.* An honest and loving (even if apprehensive) reaction that you give a thought about their safety and their future at least tells them you care. It means the world to a kid when facing an unknown future neither he nor you can fathom.

With exaggerated mimicry, I filled my journal with reactive, dramatized scrawls: "Well, Brandee." (For some reason, only my father and a few family members call me this. I personally think it sounds like I'm being called to strip on stage and hail dollar bills, but Dad liked the 70s song, and thus the name. It was an improvement on "B.J.," which I went by until I asked my mom one day why the kid up the street was calling me "blow job," and what was that? She declined to enlighten my confounded, 10-year-old mind, but knighted me Brandee that day.)

Anyway, I scrawled with the sticky ink of sarcasm my partially true and defensively embellished discussions with my dad into my journal. "Brandee, I heard the news and I just wanted to break it to ya—you you can't swing that gay thing and go to heaven, so just go ahead and stop telling people first of all. That's just embarrassing to all of us, and ya can't take it back. And now how do we get that problem fixed? Oh, well I understand you've agonized in anti-gay therapy for a year. At least you started trying. But it's clearly not successful yet, so we can send you to Evergreen, those wilderness quests, whatever it takes; we'll just have to find a way. I love ya to pieces. Here, read this and this and this. You're strong, you can resist temptation: Please stop cutting your hair, guys like long, blonde hair. Why are you giving in like this? You're my daughter, I raised you better. You're beautiful. How can you turn your back on your family, and risk your eternal soul for this debasing temptation?" These compliments were embedded with expectations, and his love felt conditional. And I was getting further and further away from meeting those conditions as I learned to be true to the real me.

I saved this clip, which Dad sent me after it was passed around as study material in his priesthood class at church. I was baffled and dismayed that "pervert" is what they were calling me. In my dad's defense, this is what they taught him in church, and he thought he was doing well to pass their opinion along to a daughter he loved and was so bewildered by.

After consideration of the evil aspects, the ugliness and prevalence of the evil of the glorious thing to remember is that it is CURABLE and forgivable. Certainly it can be overcome, for there are numerous happy people who were once involved and have since completely transformed their lives. Therefore to those who say that this practice or any other evil is incurable, I respond: "How can you say the door cannot be opened until your knuckles are bloody, till your head is bruised, till your muscles are sore? It can be done."

Many have been misinformed that they are powerless in the matter, not responsible for the tendency, and that God made them that way. This is as untrue as any other of the diabolical lies Satan has concocted. It is blasphemy. Man is made in the image of God. Does the pervert think God to be that way?

Sometimes not heavenly but earthly parents get the blame. Granted that certain conditions make it easier for one to become a pervert, but he can, if normal, rise above the frustrations of childhood and stand on his own feet.

A man may rationalize and excuse himself till the groove is so deep he cannot get out without great difficulty. But temptations come to all people. The difference between the reprobate and the worthy person is generally that one yielded and the other resisted. And if the yielding person continues to give way he may finally reach the point of no return. The spirit will not always strive with man. (D&C 1:33)

"Evergreen" is is an institution where Mormon kids who are threatening gayness go to "get the gay cleaned off." I was surprised to find that the mission statement on Evergreen's website today is very different than the old pamphlet I read in 1995. Apparently Evergreen has been criticized for its past approach and they've softened their language. Now the page reads in a more politically correct fashion:

> Since its founding more than 20 years ago as a support
> organization for the members of The Church of Jesus
> Christ of Latter-day Saints, Evergreen's mission ... is
> to assist those who experience same-sex attraction
> and who desire to live in harmony with their spiritual
> and religious values. Evergreen was founded on the
> belief that the atonement of Jesus Christ enables
> every soul the opportunity to turn away from all sins
> or conditions that obstruct their temporal and eternal
> happiness and potential.

As I've said, once inside the annals of the Mormon Church, you
cannot leave without increasing amounts of doom heaped upon your
soul. It's the perfect catch 22. If you were lucky enough to be "born
into" the church, it was because you "earned" that birthright in the
pre-life "spirit" world. If you have that privilege and you throw it
away, choosing not to live the Mormon life means you sacrifice the
happiness of your everlasting soul. This is because this life is seen,
ultimately, as a test for your placement in the afterlife. Having known
"the truth" and left the church anyway, you forfeit what you had and
then some, ending up worse off than the poor, starving Africans on
the Savannah who never heard of Mormonism. Once you're in, you are
strongly encouraged to stay in, and they don't let you out without real
effort. You have more heavenly potential, so more is expected of you.
If you leave, it's usually presumed that you are too weak to handle
the restrictions of Mormon life rather than that you are thinking for
yourself.

After over one year of struggle, during which I had been in
contact with my Logan, UT, bishop, I asked to be removed from the
church records. I knew I had tried. In spite of the gay thing, I truly
didn't believe in the exclusivity of celestial heaven and some of the
main tenets of the religion. I realized that my nature wasn't anything
to be ashamed of. The church's treatment of gays was the final blow
to an already unstable foundation of unanswered questions for me
regarding the church.

I was unmistakably gay.

At my bishop's recommendation, I had been seeing a licensed professional counselor at Utah State University for a year who was also, outside of his school counseling role, a bishop in another ward. He helped conduct the type of "anti-gay therapy" that we thought I needed. My bishop hoped he would help me be able to find a way to embrace the church's teachings in spite of the affliction I had. I gave it my best, as did the counselor, but when it didn't yield authentic results, he refused to remove me from the records when I asked him to. After all my counseling had failed to show me a reasonable and livable solution. He said I would need to go to a church court of some sort, with representation. It sounded degrading and complicated—a big, drag-on hoop to jump through. I told him I thought it was neglecting the spirit of the law, and it was ridiculous to Fort Knox my records.

I left his office for good, having first sought him out for help. Now I was finally leaving more than a little miffed at the conclusion. I continued to be sought out by Mormon missionaries who had been told to "bring me back to the fold." This carried on for the next 13 years, at over eight new residences. I would call it harassment, but the poor faces of those unknowing, often unwilling, young men were anything but the faces of someone trying to do harm. I don't think they understood how invasive it is for them to follow their orders. They are just doing what they're told, trying to be good and serve an honorable mission for the church they believe is worth serving. They didn't know I had asked the church to stop seeking me out for the millionth time. My boys, the children of my previous partner of eight years, gave them such a bad time at their final visit (asking them their feelings on gays and giving them hell for their responses), they finally made note in their records to leave us alone.

We are taught as Mormon kids that our performance in this world and through the entirety of this life determines where we are placed in one of three kingdoms. The first is the Celestial. This is the highest, most esteemed kingdom, where you can become a god or goddess yourself and your spirit lives on and loves and learns happily for eternity. You must have a heterosexual marriage in the Mormon temple and be sealed therein to achieve this highest honor. This is equivalent to uber heaven, and you will populate your own planets with your spirit children someday. You will know God, then become a God yourself. The Terrestial Kingdom holds the B- students. They weren't smoking in the back of the school, but they don't do their homework, either. They weren't praying or reading their scriptures nightly, going to church or temple regularly, etc. Half-arsed, "Jack" kind-of Mormons, I imagine. I must mention here the big, huge bunch of other "regular, good-old people" on the planet that have lived and died not having been Mormonated. The Terrestial Kingdom is where they end up if they're *pretty* good people, but not top notch. Finally (of course), there is a Telestrial, hell-type place. There has to be one of these to scare folks into better behavior, but the Mormons hold up quite shy of fire and brimstone. This is the "thinking man's hell." If you're entombed in the Telestrial Kingdom, you will remain gnashing your teeth forever, thinking of all your mistakes and regretting the decisions you made on the earth that took you away from the truth. You chose to lose the light of the church, the way and the prize, for all eternity. Time out. Go think about it. Forever.

That regret is hell enough, my father would remind me multiple times. There are no re-dos. This judgment and afterlife down-ranking is a large part of the agony Mormons feel when they know they were made differently than this model will uphold. We're flunking out through no failing of our own! What a rip off.

CHAPTER 16

SHAMELESS JESUSITA

To represent a complete contrast to me, one of my best friends announced her gayness to her Mormon family by making herself a cake. The icing exclaimed: "Congratulations, I'm Gay." She plopped the surprise gastronomical masterpiece down on the table in front of her huge family with unflinching Brazilian flair.

How dauntless is that? I couldn't identify with that at all; at the time, it was foreign to my timid, attritional, nature. "Oops. I'm sorry to be me. So sorry y'all! Can you find it deep in your hearts to tolerate my presence?". I was awe struck by Jesusita, inspired. It was reckless and irreverent awe, but awe nonetheless.

As Jesse told us her story around the table at the bar where my friends and I commonly congregated the year we all came out, we dropped our jaws in disbelief. We were slightly envious of her unrepentant composure and slightly horrified for the family, knowing how hard it is to swallow this news, even when presented as a more palatable cookie—versus cake in the face.

"You are shitting me, you liar! You did not come out to your super Mo family like that. Even *you* wouldn't go that rogue." I had to say that, but we all knew that Jess had it in her, and yeah, she probably had. I verified it with her family years later, laughing so hard I cried again imagining her poor, wide-eyed, flabberghasted mother recount the story.

As I have aged, and loved more of myself and other LGBTs, I realize: Why the heck *should* she have been apologetic? Why was I?

We shouldn't have to beg for acceptance and count ourselves lucky when our families don't abandon and expunge us from their proud crystal records. We can change our love no more than people can change the color of their skin. And why would we try when we are perfect the way we already are, in the way any person is with all their differences and quirks embraced?

I listened to her story surrounded by friends who were all living lives filled with different levels of rejection by their families. One friend was couch surfing after being kicked out of his home just for sharing with his father that he thought he *might* be gay. One friend at the table could stay at the family house, but only if she had no company over and came and went using only the back door. Another good friend—I'll call him Tim—had instantly lost all contact with his family when he came out. He never spoke much about it, even in the supportive environment we had created. It was just too painful for him, and I think it had been a surprise that his family had completely turned their backs. We all talked through our stories and offered each a shoulder, but Tim just dealt with it in silence. His eyes would well on occasion. He started drinking more, got into more serious drugs, and had shady boyfriends and acquaintances of the sort that went unintroduced, even to friends.

My friend Jesse never seemed to feel the same shame many of us did, and I always envied her moxie. She didn't comprehend why being gay would be wrong when it was just ... was. I've counted myself lucky for knowing her and her fearless, 4-foot-nothin' self assurance over the years. She frequently reminds me of the absurdity of my shame and guilt. She recently sent me a short film on YouTube, knowing I was writing this. It was so poignant I want to reference it. It's a about turning the tables on sexuality roles, and the absurdity that gay people coming out often endure when others try to convince them they're not gay.

"Are you sure? Have you just tried it? Maybe he's just not the one for you." It's by WingsSpan Pictures, and is called "Love Is All You Need." You can view it at

https://www.youtube.com/watch?v=CnOJgDW0gPI.

Jesse later went to the gynecologist's office for her very first Pap smear with heart-shaved pubes and confetti in her underwear, a treat for the gynecologist I suppose. Like I said, some days with her have been colored five shades of crazy while lost in a foreign country, but I wish I could concoct an injection of Jesse-no-shame-inspiration to share with those of you like me going through this. Find your own Jesse that gives you a vision of shameless being!

Chapter 17

Go Find Your People

Realizing that Utah was perhaps not the *most* accepting city to live in and be gay, and having met many girls who were going through the same post-Mormon torments I was, I started looking to get out. Things weren't horrible, but I still felt like a green spiky outsider with 3 eyeballs. I was walking downtown with my girlfriend one day and was hit by a bottle thrown from a car with a guy yelling something about dead dykes, for example. Events like this were always extra incentive to hit the road, though I know they could happen anywhere. The haughty, silent judgment from curch members was actually worse than the honesty of bottle hurling. I just had to believe that it was less likely to happen as often in other, select cities. I knew I could stay there and muddle through it, or high-tail it to higher ground. I had transferred to the University in Salt Lake City and got my Bachelor of Science, and become more comfortable with being gay, though still felt pretty reactive. I found a job counseling troubled youth with my Psychology degree for a couple of years before having enough saved up to join the Peace Corps. I went to Niger, West Africa and loved being out in the world—away from that oppressive feeling that I had of "otherness" at home. This is not to say that the people I met in West Africa were cool with the gays. But our skin color alone made us alien to them, so I merely switched reasons for sticking out like a sore thumb. It was no longer negative attention, just attention. After my return home early after falling ill, I started looking for a new and more accepting place to land. My previously mentioned friend Daliah had moved to Olympia, Washington, after living in Logan, and said I could rent a room in their house with her and her girlfriend, Molly. Daliah got me a job on a boat as a "sea farmer" collecting mussels with she and some friends. It was hard work outside, but stress-free and invigorating. I was still recovering from the illness that had taken me out of the Peace Corps in Niger early, and it sounded like the perfect leap to make with great people I trusted.

So I jumped out of Zion, to the great Northwest. Olympia Washington had a thriving gay culture (at least to me) that was fun and easy to get into; I was alarmed by how quickly this place felt like home more than home did. I missed my family, but I was finally feeling like it was OK to be whoever I was without worrying about what everyone else thought. I felt that I was growing comfortably into myself. I worked there for a year, applied to the University of Washington Medical School for the PA program, and got in soon after, moving up to Seattle. I met a girl I liked—I'll call her Eilan—she was quirky and smart, and we got along right away. It amazed me how great it felt to be in a relationship without trying to be anything I wasn't.

Things finally got great—Eilan had a network of wonderful and amazing people whom I soon considered my friends too. It's not hard to find your fit when you go looking in the right places. A gaggle of lesbos roving the town, finding fun things to do and great people to do it with. I had a small taste of this in Salt Lake City after coming out, but this was a jumbo sized good and happy time. I didn't feel like a freak anymore; I just felt like me—like who I *was* mattered more than whom I loved.

This continued for a long time after moving from Utah to a very gay Capitol Hill Seattle. I may have failed to mention that the gays know how to have fun like no one else with Pride, generous weekend fun and activity, and always hip and beautiful eye candy. We traveled to Dinah Shore and the White Party. Gay goodness was open, shameless, and comfortable, with multitudinous women that destroyed all stereotypes. I fit in here, and I sighed with relief knowing I wasn't the lone black unicorn. I had a blast. It was hard not to!

I no longer felt the need to try on alternate personas while looking for the me that fit. I didn't have to try so hard. I eventually left the party scene. As fun and healthy as it was in it's way, it had an expiration date like most things. I worked hard through PA school and stood more comfortably on my own two feet.

CHAPTER 18

GAYBIES

As one who freely enjoyed the nightlife and all that goes with it, I seemed to have a goal to gain an absence of unwanted emotion through drinking past moderation many times. Really, sometimes it was accidental, but there was an underlying drive I think to achieve emotional anesthesia. Though I felt I was getting over the pain and insult of my pre-Seattle life, I still had unwanted boatloads of shame and guilt that lingered in regard to who I was and where I came from. Many people can tell when the party is going too drunk: the conversations get louder and louder, tears shed, and amplified emotions above the usual response to stimuli. This used to be outrageously funny to watch as the token sober one at parties, but now that it was me joining in that behavior, it wasn't so funny. I found it embarrassing to have that lapse in conscious control, even though the release of control was what I craved.

The next morning, I would usually beat myself up unnecessarily-ok the the next day, er week (why let Catholic guilt pass Mormon guilt by? Let's be honest about the ever-constant, undying guilt). I'd awake with a bass drum accompanied hangover in my head and a mental laundry list of regret for what happened when I let go. As I said, I wasn't always my best self, but the religious guilt was always worse than the reality of what really happened: the dancing on a table, swimming naked in freezing Lake Union, or crying out my unfiltered feelings on a topic of universal or religion-based despair.

My guilt was always out of proportion to the offense, shoot I had guilt for the simple fact of letting go my tight control. No one ever resented me like *I* resented me for the usual drunken spillings and laughable retractions in the wake of what everyone knows was an annebriated occasion. Most often I was a happy "I love you man" drinker, who happened to be a titch of a control freak in my waking conscious life, so couldn't find peace with this "letting go" behavior I apparently needed on occasion.

Drugs? Not so much. I once spent half an hour looking for my car keys under a coffee table after trying some tame marijuana at my girlfriend's house for the first time, so paranoid that I was positive that someone had stolen them. Because my twenty year old light blue Ford Fairlane was such a hot commodity, I really had to be careful to keep an eye on those keys. I can be a perfectly competent jackass on my own, thank you very much. I don't need the help of any other substances to amplify my natural abilities. After a few other things I tried went just as well, I decided to steer clear entirely.

I also tried to be dynamic in relationships, and to date multiple people, to stay unconnected to just one person in a big, new, gay city and "see all that was out there," but I sucked at that too. I was a stereotypical serial monogamist lesbo, and promiscuity wasn't my style, either. Though I tried. I tried to learn from the best gay men in the city, but I wasn't interested without a real relationship underlying the action.

My exuberation came and stuck around past the great Seattle night life. The second best thing about being in an accepting culture: When I would say I was gay to straight coworkers, they never batted an eye. I could tell they weren't continuing to uncomfortably force conversation after I just dropped an awkward bomb on their chat pattern. They just didn't really care!

I became single again, and reconnected with an old acquaintance and we started dating. I knew I wanted family, and Yvonne already had two beautiful boys I had the pleasure of helping to raise from the time they were eight and nine years old. She had the children during troubled teenage years and had been raising them alone. I thought that would feed the desire to have kids that I had. What else was I going to do, start a family? Get sperm donors and sci-fi myself a baby with beakers, microscopes, and intrauterine injections? (Snort laugh. Seriously. Beam me up, Scotty). I suggested *me* having a baby once to Yvonne in trying to figure out an end to my unexplained feeling of longing and malcontent. She couldn't even *pretend* to entertain the idea, cracking up and incredulously alluding to the teenaged antics we were going through with the boys at the time. It was understandable from her point of view, she had been there and done that and the boys were teenaged nightmares for a few years. So we stayed together a little too long. Happy for a long time, but then slowly not-so-happy, devolving to miserably unfulfilled and moderately wretched at the end, without the connection we both longed for. I loved those boys, but I knew it wasn't the same as having my own. They were getting older and already going off to do their own thing. I was very confused, as I had really loved her, and always probably would, I just didn't want to be with her anymore and nothing made sense.

By this time, I thought the perfect relationship was a Sasquatch.

I imagined myself out there, doing whatever I wanted as a single person, with no strings attached. This was incredibly refreshing for someone used to a life of heavy responsibilities for a while, and then ... I felt a sucking black hole of weepy regret. I was terrified. Living life with no kids and without someone who got me, grew me, and pushed for the most out of life with me? I had really loved Yvonne, but we hadn't been able to grow together. Though I knew that to be true, I missed the life we had made. I missed the best friend I lost in her her too. I was glad I was in their lives and I was grateful for the often loving, always growth-inducing, and sometimes challenging relationship we all had. The idea felt like an empty track on the path I had navigated, nothing more than working, making more money, waiting for the next cool event or party to attend that just created more longing in the end. Continue in a life-sucking career? Develop hobbies? More travel? Then what? It just wasn't for me without a loving partner and a family. Growing up in a big Mormon household had primed me for it, I suppose. It felt like rain sucking at my slow, drained tires, like I just couldn't get traction or steer my own life because I was hypnotized into believing the old-fashioned gay myth. When you're gay, you sacrifice having kids. That's the trade-off. You are a big plug in the evolutionary, reproductive bathtub. You love someone without the required plumbing, so you have a kid-shaped gash in your big gay heart. Additively, I had the hapless mindset that empowered me to remain adrift, without the wherewithal to take a good honest look at what I was, what I wanted, and make a map of how to get there. It felt empty but I didn't have the guts yet to assert what I wanted. Not even to my own conscious mind. It just seemed so contrived and far-fetched to orchestrate the making of a happy family and having a child in my circumstance.

Finally the breakup with Yvonne came, uglier than I would have liked from having waited too long, but after a year we were able to be friends again, which I value greatly. Xijo has always remained a part of my life in Seattle, and I am filled with pride whenever I see him, and to watch him with my kids now is like a crazy full circle of life.

I finally got my shizzle together and found enough hope to keep looking eventually. In the wrong place. Did I mention after I said I was not a real writer that I am also not a quick study or a role model? If I omitted that, (now that we are more than halfway through) I apologize if you hoped for more. If you have an appreciation for boneheaded jackassery, however, then read on with delight please.

I tried to date a guy again, thinking maybe I had changed out of dismayed grief, or at my furthest mental reach, that at least I could have a child the old-fashioned way, chanting to myself: "Love doesn't work anyway! All women are crazy (myself included)! What have I got to lose? At least I'd be with a nice enough guy, and have kids to show for it". Shame. I knew better, but that's how deeply I lost myself and questioned everything about my life after the end of my long relationship that I thought would last. My hard head had to re-live my late teenage years again, as if once isn't one time too many.

My guy was kind, classy, and a gentleman through and through. My conspiring friends and I dubbed him the Italian Stallion. He was literally gorgeous (I have no idea how I landed him), and happy to help with my "playing it straight" experiment. I was completely honest with him, and in the end it once again proved the point that you can't change your sexuality for all the want you can muster. There was no fairy tale swap to straight-ville for me, no matter the quality of the man.

After this illuminating exercise in futility, I boxed up the kid and relationship idea, duct taped it and stuffed it in the back of my mind's dark basement. I was convinced that it was never going to happen. By this time I was no spring chicken at 35 years old, single, jaded, and unsure of myself. How could anyone resist this package? No clue.

I fumbled around, aimlessly dating randomly for what felt like forever. Old friends I shouldn't mix lines with? Super! Date colleagues in the workplace where it may create extreme discomfort if (when) things don't go ideally? Brilliant! Bring on the train wrecks! Who knows, my antics may entertain an audience of readers one day? Any other life-hijack catastrophies I could drum up seemed to be magnetized to my person, like I was transmitting out to the Universe "Hey, let's see how messy this can get". My life had big missing chunks, like I'd crossed the line at a shotgun shooting range and stood in for target practice, and I just kept stumbling along like a bellicose, disoriented zombie. I had a fancy job in cardiac surgery as a PA that made my stomach clench with tension every time I went to work in the operating room or the cardiac intensive care unit, but it "looked" like success so I couldn't bring myself to leave. Also, they gave me money, and I needed that. I still didn't even have the guts to consciously put a finger of what I wanted for my life, let alone try to manifest it. If you don't want to be disappointed, don't have any expectations, right?

Then Nicole happened.

CHAPTER 19

U-HAULED

We met courtesy of the luckiest email I've ever written (framed on our wall, entitled, "Too little, too late?"). It landed me a low-expectations date with this woman who had been emotionally crushed by her ex-partner of ten years—after having a child together. My heart ached for her, as she relayed this without even the attempt at hiding the anger that still burned beneath her cool surface.

I had said "no kids" in my online dating profile, but she had reached out to me anyway. I dallied about six weeks before remembering to get back to her after canceling our first date due to being on call and having to go in last minute to assist in an emergency surgery. I no longer subscribed to the short-lived dating service after a night of horrors with a woman who looked so unlike her online picture I walked by her twice at the bustling little restaurant we were meeting at. Okay, I understand the tendency to submit your very best picture to represent yourself, though it's not entirely true to form. A "skinny, good hair day" picture in your prime, perfect lighting overlooking any wrinkles, and perhaps taken before any of those little gray hairs started sprinkling your crown. This is normal. The picture she posted was not her. That's not normal. Second "not normal" was that she was much more attractive than the picture she had posted. Who does that? Was she in the witness protection program? CIA? A pathological liar? Once she had evidently decided she wasn't going to ditch me, she came over to say hello and led me, bewildered, to our table. It was about five minutes into the usual get to know you chit-chat when I realized that she was on a full-steam crazy train. I started playing an internal game of "diagnose that personality disorder", which was super fun until her stories really came alive and she attracted spooked and disapproving looks from the people around us, banging on our table and raising her voice to a level usually reserved for small children approaching full-blown tantrum. I ordered a second beer and an appetizer instead of an entrée, and excused myself to the restroom. When I returned, she had found personality number three, and began quizzing me as to why I took my purse to the bathroom. She loudly dubbed me mistrustful and horrible on the spot, and she expected an apology. I stammered something like "Sometimes a girl just needs her purse when using the loo." I implied, eyebrows elevated, that perhaps I needed some lady products and it was my time of the month. It wasn't true, but the suggestion worked and she resumed nice personality number one as my deodorant waved the white flag and I started scoping the emergency exit door hungrily. After rearranging my appetizer around my plate a few times, I said I had to pay my meter and ducked behind my steering wheel as I drove out of the parking lot, praying she wouldn't see me.

On my next and final date, I found myself bobbing haplessly on a very nice girl's very broken boat in the middle of Lake Washington. This woman had never driven the very, very used boat before, and had just purchased it. She seemed very proud of her adventurous spirit, and said she had read that I liked boating on my profile, so thought it would be cool. She sat in the boat eating a lovely picnic she had prepared, thoroughly enjoying herself for two hours while I flagged down strangers for a tow. Hilarious. After we were back on land, it was *so* hilarious.

I returned home and closed my match.com account as fast as my fingers could type "Dear Lord, I give up and will happily live single forever just let it be over".

My friends thought I was making it up, just trying to top my last story in the spirit of entertaining embellishments. Needless to say, I was hesitant to engage again with anyone I had come into contact with through match after this. Having cancelled our first date, though, I felt I at least owed this Nicole person a drink and an apology. I knew she had arranged for a babysitter for our previously arranged night and it was a bit of a last minute cancel. Against my better judgement and out of pure unadulterated guilt, I suggested that we meet out for a drink. A nice, safe, single beverage, after which time there was no obligation, and I could escape.

The day came, and I showed up looking like something the cat dragged in. I had just been at a pool party I didn't want to leave, and having cancelled on her once before, I felt too flaky doing it again. So I delayed getting ready for our date to stay at the pool for another hour. I showed up with low expectations and mostly wet, chlorinated hair, no belt with pants 2 sizes too big (the result of my depression diet), no earrings, no make-up, and wet socks that had fallen in the pool as I reluctantly scurried off. When I saw her I instantly felt sheepish. She seemed... normal. A little slick in her black leather jacket, but surprisingly sans psychiatric disorders.

After apologizing for being my usual five to ten minutes late and looking like a brewing vagrant with stolen clothing and questionable intentions, we launched into easy conversation. We spoke so easily and frankly about our recent experiences that it felt like we were skipping over the first, second, and fourth date scenarios to just get to the point and know all there was to know about each other. Her voice was tinged with hope, and she sat on a smile and a laugh ready for quick release, just waiting for a reason. We didn't want to waste time with "near misses", and she had had unpleasant dating scenarios and had left the dating service as well. Our drink turned in to dinner and an extended walk around Seattle's beautiful Queen Anne neighborhood, with the squish of my wet socks in my Converse nearly gone by the time we parted. We noticed it was dark and many hours had passed, but both of us seemed to dread departure.

I was impressed that even after being as devastated as she was, Nicole had a vitality and optimistic outlook on life that I fell in love with on that night. She had a feverish integrity and a can-do spirit that was obviously immutable in spite of her previous partner and the terrible experience she had been through. I was entranced. She admitted she was at her life's lowest, and I marveled that she was still this shining, buoyant light. No-nonsense intelligent, green glittery-eyed, lovely and gracious. This was scary in that I knew I was experiencing the beginning of something I could only hope to be ready for, having just started emerging from a very solid post-breakup, sowing-wild-oats moronic phase.

True to lesbian stereotype, we were joined at the hip from our second date forward. We didn't "technically" move in together for six months, but we referred to my downtown apartment appropriately as "the storage unit". She proposed after six months.

What does a lesbian bring on a first date?

A U-haul.

Nicole became the "carrot" I didn't think existed, making the journey worth every bit of the struggle. I adore her and the relationship we have made. Every day since our fateful "ugly duckling from the pool date", I have felt the gratitude of one who knows they stumbled onto greatness, teetering on the cusp o' radiance. I regained the hope in all things higher that I had lost. I started working toward my higher self, took inventory, and got to work moving forward again. I stopped trying to drink away sadness, which had always just created more sadness, with a side order of shame and regret soup. I reconnected with the guide I had missed having in my life. I started delving in to ways to reconnect with God, or Source, or whatever you want to call it, in the absence of organized religion. I listened to so many hours of Deepak Chopra on my audible account, I took on an Indian accent. I left my soul-sucking job for less money and more satisfaction. I connected with my patients and realized that I belonged in a life of service, not status. I came out of my fog and started charting goals mindfully instead of drifting to where the wind blew.

I look forward to every day I have with her. She gets me, and anchors me, and urges me to grow to my potential. We appreciate our differences instead of tolerating them. We laugh with each other and at each other. We teach each other things we are learning on our own, read and discuss new and interesting books together, raise our kids, figure out life's problems, and come up with ways to fix what needs fixing together. She is the most self-disciplined person I have ever known, and I have an endless amount of respect for her. She is worth every lonely, scary day that I struggled through.

CHAPTER 20

BABY MAKIN'

You may be checking pages for the chapters in between meeting Nicole and here, explaining how Nicole and I fell deeper into love, walked on beaches, met each other's families, and started considering commitment more seriously. After which time, after long and responsible deliberation we would decide to get married. A year later we would trepidatiously start discussing the baby makin'. Well, you didn't miss any chapters. It happened so fast, it doesn't even get it's own chapter. Here's a paragraph:

When I met her I felt like I already knew her, and she me. All our fun and weird and broken and awesome parts fit together. We were immediately in love and within 6-9 months we lived together, got married, and were trying to get pregnant. Without any problem blocking out the horrified, apprehensive guffaws of those reasonable, responsible people surrounding us. Which was everyone, except our sisters pretty much.

So, back to baby-makin'. The whole idea was totally Star-Trek contrived and foreign to me, but Nicole brought it crashing down to earth and into my uterus without giving a lot of time to overthink it. She has clear goals and a drive to accomplish them without hesitation once her mind is made up, a quality I aspire to. When had I started to let fear of what others thought influence my choices in life, especially such a massive choice? All my fears and stereotype aversions were vanquished when I was honest with myself about really wanting this, coupled with her persistent optimism and energetic drive. We picked a sperm donor very much like her. It felt right from the start, like we were on a motorized, guided airport path. I was "letting" my life happen as it should, instead of trying so hard to force it.

My heart was so full of love for our daughter, my wife, and my extended family before our darling son finally arrived, I couldn't conceive of how there would be any room for more love in my life. From the moment he was delivered into my arms, I felt a ferocious, explosive love for him I never knew could exist. And there's sudden, expansive space for all of it! I thought I had understood all the accounts of parents doing anything in the world for their children, but I didn't yet fully comprehend emotionally. Becoming a parent is truly indescribable (though it isn't stopping me from trying, is it?). He has bonded our family even closer with a big personality to rival his big sister's. I can't imagine going through my life without him. He truly is the light of my life, outside of his unnatural lack of requirement for sleep, and my subsequent perpetual half-lidded fatigue, and I hope I can encourage all of you who want children and are trepidatious as I was. Don't rob yourself of the experience of parental love if that's what you want for anything! I can't think of anything more heartbreaking than having lived my life without having him because I was scared or what people would say, how we would be judged, or didn't like the idea of the difficult or expensive process, or even the donor conundrum. If you wait until everything is "perfect", you could be waiting forever. Jump in and trust that the Universe makes things happen as they should, and I feel at the right time. Just try, start the ball rolling, do your part, and know that you and all of your imperfections and flaws are also part of what can make you a great parent.

As an aside, these usually young donors who are willing to help families who don't have the ability to conceive children readily do so with such kindness and good intent, I was utterly blown away! One guy wrote, "I grew up with steps and half's and full siblings, and I learned that family is who you love, no matter the genetic parents.

If I can help people out there be happy who really want a child and would raise it with love, I am happy to."

Another donor candidate wrote, "I want to give families who can't otherwise have kids the opportunity to have what I had growing up—an extended, loving family, genetically related or not." I want all of those kind men to know they bring joy to the lives of parents and the other kids who become their siblings. For minimal financial benefit, you've given us a lifelong and amazing gift. And for those donors willing to meet their child when they turn 18, even more thanks. This may not always be an easy thing to explain to a spouse or kids of your own down that you may have down the road, but it has incredible value for a child to be able to see their genetic contributor.

CHAPTER 21

AFTER MY FATHER'S ALIEN ABDUCTION

After our son was born, my father came to stay with us for a week. This is something he had never done before and had never even threatened. Previously when visiting Washington, he would stay with a friend of his just outside of Seattle and would meet us for outings instead, able to retreat to sinless safety when he saw fit. We were all comfortable with that level of overlap.

My father and I had made amends a few years prior, discussing what had happened to our relationship with open candor. He sincerely apologized for turning his back on me during a time when I really needed a parent's example and support. He had been a young father working his way through graduate school while supporting four children. He was big enough to admit that he had used my gayness, and the embarrassment that I was to him, to stop the already minimal financial support he had been giving me in college. He was always budgeted to-the-quick, and the money he saved by cutting me off gave him some financial cushion. So he took it and left me to my own devices.

He wasn't proud of this, and I was really touched by the regret I knew he felt in admitting it to me in order to make sincere reparations. He was tearful, contrite, and honest, and I really appreciated that. He said he hadn't intended to humiliate me or make me feel worse by sending virtual boatloads of anti-gay gear to my dorm; he was just trying to save my soul like he thought he was supposed to. It takes a big person to own up to that. I remember getting his phone call in the Home Depot parking lot, then sitting in my car for an hour trying to digest his perspective, thinking of what this repaired relationship would mean in my life. We had been estranged for well over ten years! I didn't have a slot in my mind or in my life anymore for all things *dad*. I didn't agree with his actions, but now I could at least understand some of the undercurrent of his motives. He didn't do what he did to hurt me, and he relayed that he just didn't understand me, and didn't know what to do. I feel better at peace than at war even if I feel I'm justified to hold a grudge, and forgiveness felt like a wave of relief.

I was surprised to see how quickly we moved to put our differences aside and let bygones be bygones, harboring no resentments as long as we don't talk about politics. He was a good person who had always tried to do what he thought was right. He was fun to be around, good-natured, and I had missed him. I had pulled away and made myself unavailable to him as soon as I feared he was rejecting me, so I didn't make it easy to relate to me at that time either. I really worked to let go of my old walls around him. It was hard to do, after learning to live with the idea that I lost him and I didn't need him to be happy, but I decided to incorporate him into my life on some level. I wanted my kids to have the kind, thoughtful, and loving grandfather that he would be to them.

I was more than a little nervous with him coming to stay, but happy that he wanted to bond with our kids. Above the mantle over our fireplace, we had a large picture on canvas from our commitment ceremony (before marriage was legal in Washington). It's of the back of Nicole and me holding hands in front of our lovely Reverend, whom we were fortunate enough to have join us at our legal marriage a few years later. Just as the picture was taken, our daughter bounded in just between us and plopped on the floor as if staged.

I caught my father staring at the photo from the first ceremony multiple times during his stay. Just before he left, after a heartfelt and sweet visit with him, he turned to me with real tears in his crinkly blue eyes and said,

"Well, Brandee, I'm proud of ya. I can't say I believe that what you have here is wrong. In fact, I find myself looking at you and your little family and feeling like I wish I had that love for myself. It's beautiful. I don't claim to totally understand God and all His ways, but there's a lot of love here, and I'm thankful to know you have it in your life. I love ya to death, babe."

I answered, "Who are you, and what have you done with my father?" I didn't know how to react to this sweet man in my old dad's skin.

I expected a visit from a generally well-meaning man who I cared about but who didn't accept me, and I expected him to pepper in comments reflecting what I'm sure a lot of people think but don't say: "A boy's gonna need a father."

"Who will teach him how to pee?"

"Who's he gonna talk to about the birds and the bees, heh?"

As if we are not complete—not up to the task of raising a penis-possessing child with just love and vulvas floating around, all aflutter with no direction to point the boy in. "Who will throw a football with him?"

To these unspoken comments I would retort: Hulloooo. ... We're gay girls. We love to throw or kick or bounce or volley any kind of ball, especially when it means *not* having to do other more gender-specific girl things. I'm sorry to be stereotypical, but in our case the perpetuated stereotype is true as it is in many.

The point being, our son will see some games and play sports aplenty. And he'll have his share of male influences to talk to whilst running and crushing opponents in a testosterone-rich environment if he so chooses.

But to be fair to all kinds of parents out there: even if he didn't, so what?

Lots of dads don't do that stuff. I know some straight dads that can barely walk and talk at the same time, let alone catch a ball hurtling through space toward their person, and they are devoted and loving fathers. Loads of kids and their parents have *no* common interests (e.g., my cheerleading, singing, homecoming-queening mom and me). Unfortunately many more kids are lucky these days to have even *one* parent who is lovingly invested in them. Every person needs good role models, especially when they're young, but those don't necessarily need to be grounded in common interests. Sometimes that model is a parent and many times it isn't, but the most important virtues and lessons in life don't all have to do with the gender or hobbies of the one who is teaching. The responsibility to have good men and women around for our son to choose from falls on us, and we'll make that happen.

I think the point is that unconditional love, direction, good examples, consistent involvement and understanding of what the kid wants in life, is going to make a kid well adjusted and happy if the kid is willing to let it be so. Call me crazy.

There will likely be times that he will wish he had a father for various reasons, and we will do our best with that situation when it arises. I sometimes felt that way after my parents divorced and I *had* a known father. I relied on the people I had access to, and it was plenty.

Do I think I'm doing my son a disservice bringing him into the world without a dad? Not this kid. He is the happiest, most loved little man I know. All banging, hugging, stomping, loud, sweet celebrated boy surrounded by people who love him, male and female. Without motherly bias, I think he is going to be able to make anything out of his life that he chooses to, with all the tools gained in childhood and, God-willing, the confidence and skills to do so.

I never had occasion to use the defensive rant in my head that I spent way too much time thinking of while mentally preparing for Dad's visit. I didn't need it, because his heart—or the spirit—had already spoken to him more clearly than I ever could.

What I expected and what I experienced of my father were so divergent I had to pinch myself. This was a changed man, softened and wise in his nearly 70 years. Perhaps having six very different children and two humbling divorces helped. Somehow his feeling of what is right and wrong eventually overcame what a book or a church leader once told him. He retrained his faith that it would all be okay with God in the end because God is just and loving. This is something I never thought I would hear from him in my life. I think it means infinitely more to me now because *he* changed his harsh and painful judgment of gays, or all "others," because of Nicole and me.

Maybe I was born my father's child in order for him to overcome his anti-gay bias. And he's part of the reason I have gained back my faith in the overcoming, unsinkable goodness of the people in this world. To practice the art of true forgiveness. I do believe anyone can change for the better. If you are going through this, or have already, don't give up hope. You may have people in your life you think will never change. If they are willing to have any interaction, give them the chance to do what they're comfortable doing to stay in touch;

they may not be able to see you with a partner for a while, but keep the door open if you care about that relationship. It can get better, no matter how opposed they are.

I saw my dad break away from dictated views and think for himself, allowing himself to feel what he did, not what he "should." In those moments I had with him, and in sweet phone calls and interactions since, I found myself so grateful for the change. I had my dad back.

He told me, when I asked him for the purposes of this book, what had caused his change of heart on the issue.

First, he listed me. Many of you reading this are doing so because a friend or loved one has come out, and you're trying to understand them better, or get a grasp on what they're going through and why. This is the most common impetus for change of heart.

Second, he got to know "a gay guy" pretty well, who had rented a room in his house. They had gotten to know each other well and had long talks about how he knew he was gay and how it felt for him when he realized it and how hard he had tried to change it. Once it really sunk in for my father that we LGBT's don't choose our sexuality, and we certainly can't change it, he felt that it wasn't fair to judge someone because of it. He said there were things that he couldn't understand or explain in God's world, but he could empathize with and have compassion for those who were different; that he knows God is good and just in the end. I don't want to speculate or overstep relaying Dad's feelings, so I'll quote this unprompted text message he recently sent:

> I've got to come up there and see you guys. I need to have a relationship with that little guy and your daughter, too. I know there are answers that are not available to us yet for reasons known only to God. There is no doubt that God loves you, and I know the trials you went through concerning the gay situation. I know that you and Nicole are good people, wonderful people. I know that your son was part of

our family before he came to this world so there has to be a plan. I know there is, and I know that it will all be OK someday and both of you will be with us in the end. When I pray for you in the mornings as I pray for everyone in the family, I feel peace. I do not feel turmoil, and I receive assurance from the Lord that things will be just fine. I have had enough experience with prayer and how God answers my prayers to know that He is telling me this. I love you all so much as I do all my children, and I am looking forward to spending eternity with all of you. If we all continue to do our best, I have no doubt this will happen. For now, sweetheart, be happy.

My father is not throwing up his hands, saying, "All is good for the gays; say sorry and bring 'em into the fold! Where's the cake and confetti?" But he now believes whatever God is out there will get it right somehow in the end, and that's huge. No, it's *ginormous*. This is a man who sent me hulking *boxes* of humiliating, anti-gay literature. He sent excerpts from church talks about my "perversion," with admonitions to fight temptation until my hands were figuratively bloody. He hardly spoke to me for years from disappointment and embarrassment. Now, he sends my wife a text message congratulating her after the supreme court ruling on gay marriage and tells her how much he loves her.

Dad, I hope when the aliens took you, the probes didn't cause permanent damage. Really, I do love, admire and appreciate you. I know you did your best and I hope your words help another parent out there find the grace you've found on this truly conflict ridden topic in the church.

If my previously recalcitrant father has made this 180 degree transition to having a loving and open approach to gays, and having faith in his maker that it will all work out, be encouraged that your struggling, religious loved ones can do it too. You can build a boatload of hope that those around you can and will change their hearts. Give them the time they need to make the turn. Stick with your values, be your best person, and love whom you love with integrity. If your family is worth their salt, they will know *through you* that who you are is alright, and change. If not, you likely won't miss that kind of person in your life in the long run.

My dad was never so great to me as at the moment of his text to Nicole, and I never loved him so much. I knew he had stretched so far to have that perspective. We had come further than I ever thought possible.

CHAPTER 22

TAKE IT FROM THE SOURCE (BRACE YOURSELF FOR THE WOO-WOO)

I want to share with you some alternative spiritual insights, resources, and resonant guidance I have found over the years. I think it's relevant here only because so many of us leaving the church feel like we have to lose our spiritual link to God, and don't' know where else to look for it when they leave. It's a link that you don't want to lose, and it's not branded to the LDS church or any other.

So how, might you ask, am I now *so* sure that God doesn't bow to a religion's rules, and loves blindly? What makes me think I know anything special about God at all?

Valid question! I searched a very long time to find the answer I could really trust with both my intellect and my intuition when I had a spiritual tug of war going on in my head. I sometimes felt I couldn't be trusted due to the power of my rationalizing, sneaky subconscious. I wanted an obvious and infallible answer, for instance, the Angel Moroni atop the temple trumpeting the answer across the valley would have worked. Vegas style instructive blinking lights would have also been sufficient. Is that so much to ask?

After years of digging around on my own, I found two convincing solutions. First solution; do experiments! Treat life like a science project, even your spiritual life. You can test out this higher power's existence- one great way is mapped out in a book by Pam Grout called E2. It's astounding and convincing, and you should have no apologies for wanting your higher power to step up and be seen. The second solution was to get a source of information that was incontrovertible. Seeking out the stories of people who had died and had actually seen what it's like after leaving the earth and their bodies, and who have come back to tell about it. Those who have experienced near death experiences (NDEs) and returned with stories of what happens after they leave are, to me, the most valuable and believable accounts of what to expect and what their experience of God was. I thought this was the closest thing to the horse's mouth I could get! If you want to know what Switzerland is like, do you ask someone who has been to Switzerland, or someone who read a big book about Switzerland?

There are numerous accounts of people who have had NDEs, returning back to life to tell the tales of what they experienced. Most of their stories align and support very similar feelings and experiences without deviation, so I'd like to share with you the things that helped me integrate the religion of my upbringing and the spiritual path that I feel is the most beneficial for me and I believe can be to many others. I will attempt to gracefully recount and avoid plagiarizing what I have gleaned in general.

Most the NDE stories come with lots of "going toward the light" stories, just like Carol Ann in Poltergeist, with great consistency from one story to the next. Baths of light and love all around, even given to beings who reportedly lived very flawed lives.

The most touching accounts do not denounce or affirm any religion or dogma whatsoever. The consistency of stories spans culture and religion, and not one NDE account relays that rules, punishments, and a certain denomination is imperative to enlightenment and joining the Universal love that God is after we leave this world. Lutherans don't get a silver medal second to Muslims, while the rest of God's children get benched for missing the "right religion" boat entirely.

Learn to love each other! Not just the ones that are beautiful and charming and easy to love, love *everyone*. God is *not* judgy. You don't have to earn his love, you are adored just because you are a spark of him/herself born into a human body. We are all one as members of humanity. We're all small parts of the greater whole, and separation from your source and each other is an illusion we only see in this life, and it's the reason for a great deal of sorrow.

Seek and find joy, be happy and kind. Enjoy the sensory and interpersonal opportunity that life is while you are here. No, don't be a gluttonous train wreck, but do stop and enjoy the pleasures in life while you're here.

In my favorite account by Anita Moorjani in her book Dying to be Me, she beautifully states that the love she felt from her Source during her NDE experience was unconditional, and that she now understands that she actually *is* God. God is *in* all of us, and we are our own source and cannot be separated from it. We can squash it down, stomp on it, hide it and mute it, but not lose it. Our goals in this world are to learn to love each other, but the biggest challenge is to truly love *ourselves*. How we come to *not* love ourselves is a bit of a mystery in this physical world. Carolyn Myss, the great medical intuitive and teacher, says that we all have to learn self-esteem in this life in order to achieve our great callings, but we don't come with it installed. You alone have the power to reorganize your world by taking the reins and becoming who you want to be; steering where your life is going. It's amazing how many of us feel victim to circumstances and powerless to change our thinking that perpetuates the circumstances. More and more substantiated research is showing that changing the thoughts you think can literally change world you live in, as well as transform your own physical health.

This completely cooked my noodle, and is fascinating to think about. My mind is blown when I listen to her story, where Anita actually dies of the cancer that had ravaged her body with tumors the size of lemons. In the next world, she was given the choice to return or stay. She was urged to return by her deceased father on the other side, and in so choosing, she knew that when she returned she would heal the broken body she had left somehow. And it happened! Huge tumors, gone-zo. Doctors were unable to show what caused her rapid, spontaneous, and complete remission. She is a living miracle, cancer free and full of life. And enjoying many more of life's little pleasures, like chocolate, since the experience.

The thing that made returning to this life tolerable for her (no one seems to want to come back after experiencing the other side), was that the knowledge that the "heaven" she felt there isn't really an outside place. It's not an address in a place far outside of our galaxy. It is a state of mind; a state of existence that she could bring back with her. Her other poignant observation about this existence was that if we will inspect our motives for all the things we do in order to know if it comes from a place of fear or of passion, we can create an elevated life worth living. It leads to us acting out of our higher self's potential instead of trying to please the people around us. We don't necessarily need someone else to tell us how to behave or what to do, though it's nice to have role models. We don't benefit from believing what someone tells us about being judged based on one of hundreds of religious or other belief systems. All we have to do is learn to fine tune our own intuition and listen to our highest selves. Seek out the best good people and environments, surround yourself with them, and give back your highest good in return. We came to our world and our bodies with a built in barometer for our own truth. Trusting this is freaky, and the batteries on the barometer I have need frequent replacements.

As I have studied these concepts and tried to apply them over time, I've found this to be incredibly difficult, but entirely true and worth practicing. Everything we aspire to be and everything we love is already packed into us. We don't have to search outside ourselves. No spiritual quests to high mountains in Nepal, weekly church meetings, or exhaustive pilgrimage to holy cleansing places are required for enlightenment, though they can be beneficial. I have found many wonderful teachers, elevated signposts to truth or beacons from above, who can show us that there is a feasible and tangible way to help uncover what we have forgotten, and learn to follow our intuition in honoring it.

Any Buddhist teachings that are consistent with the true tenets of the philosophy are incredibly helpful as a final tip to anyone still reading who is curious. It's not so much a religion as a practice, and hard to employ all the time in day to day life, but masters such as Pema Chodron bring the concepts down to earth and are incredibly enlightening. The things you can accomplish through meditation are surprising and definitely worth investigation.

Because we are all so unique with different things to learn in our lifetimes, no blanket structural rules can be right for everyone. Yeah, there are universal truths of course, like "don't kill people and be jerkweeds", but duh. We can do better than that! We need to be kind to others and internally kinder to ourselves. We should have less negative self-talk, and restrict our souls less in areas where we are learning to be greater and to fulfill our potential progress. We are supposed to make mistakes, and to explore, admire, and appreciate more of our bodies, souls, and our unique gifts as well as our challenges. That means big fat floppy failures as well! Brené Brown's enlightening TED talk and books on her research in the field of vulnerability, courage, shame and empathy show how risk is integral to growth and the full human experience. I'm sure you have heard stories of the Wright brothers failing miserably multiple times at making a hunk of metal fly, and that most of their town shunned them in embarrassment by the time they made history. But people can still be so reticent to try something amazing for fear of failing! It seems to me that caring so much about what anyone thinks that we won't risk looking like a failure is directly linked to a life of mediocrity at best. And this is the way the greatest percentage of the world lives! We can be so much more!

Another tip from Moorjani is the relationship our spirit and body have to each other- just like there can be "issues in the tissues", there can be great wisdom in our bodies to teach us if we can learn to listen to it, to harness and control it's energy for great benefit. If the religion that you ascribe to puts rules on you that make you feel anything other than uplifted and inspired, loved and celebrated, then of what good is it? If it uplifts you and others around you, then embrace it! Religion can be a magnificent catalyst for goodness and healthy community. The messages from Moorjani and many others like her support what I learned the hard way through my life. We all have our own personal spiritual paths where we learn how to tap into spirit, and trust our own unique selves. Here's what I feel I can't fairly rephrase with the same feeling as she portrayed, so I quote:

> "If we simply live in a way that nurtures us, and allows us to express our creativity, letting us see our own magnificence, that's the best we can possibly do. To advocate any option or doctrine as being the only one true way would only serve to limit who we are and what we've come here to be."

It's helped me immensely to stay open minded in my search for betterment, and keep an eye to it however I mindfully can.

"We don't have to actually work at doing anything, like following specific rituals or dogma to stay in touch with our magnificence. We can if we want to, if it brings us pleasure to do so. But it's not a requirement. Simply by following our internal guidance, we find what's right for us including the methodology we used to look for it. We know we're on the right track when we feel ourselves at the center of our love without judgment of ourselves or others and we recognize our true magnificence when within the infinite whole."

We Mormons had a big dose of faith teaching as children, and now we can apply it in a direction that provides not only comfort in return, but life changing, powerful outcomes.

If I can remember to consciously live each moment internally, thinking of the soul who's really in there instead of an external observer, my life works. Meditation, prayer, and metaphysical evaluation help immensely to surrender mental control to your heart, or at least partner with it. Of all that I have read and learned to apply, I most highly recommend this as life changing. Dr. Joe Dispenza and Deepak Chopra beautifully outline step by step how to make meditation a reality in life instead of a lofty unattainable concept, for reference.

We are born as little clean slates, still with the memory of spirit in us, but we have the world of our parents to look to and a world with rules and a narrow margin of what acceptability is and how to achieve the best life within this window. Then, as we progress through life, we go backward again. We question "Why did I ever think that way was 'the' way?" If I trust in something higher than me, and I know that something exists, then I can align myself with the goodness that vibes from it, and amazing things will happen, just not in the way I always want or expect. But contrary to the way I was taught, I don't have to control everything. I can let go the white knuckled reins and melt into the faith that things work out. Yes, I must still do the work, I must map my dreams, have clear intentions and work hard toward my goals. No one outside your highest self is going to get you out of bed and tell you what your heart wants most! When you learn that you are great, learn what your greatest gift is, and decide to run with it, Spirit will always be the wind at your back. Your linear A to B thinking has to make room for the other 24 letters that may or may not be involved. I know for a fact that the things I've done so far in my life that are consistent with my best self, were not done by me alone. And when I was pushing myself in an "I should" direction, not "I really would love to" direction, I always hit walls.

There are many more sources grounded in science that have made the difference in my ability to spiritually progress without the persisting religiously fed fear that I'm probably off to hell after all this is said and done. Skip this if it's not your bag, these are just groundbreaking teachers I found that gave me a catapult to social and spiritual self-understanding that I am happy to share. We live in an amazing time, with groundbreaking spiritually related study and leadership available if you go looking.

Neuroanatomist Dr. Jill Bolte Taylor outlines the incredible details of her stroke at the age of 37. Her accounting helped me (start to) internalize that we are all one, and not separate from each other or from God. This is oh-so hard to swallow as a new concept, and when some people I meet make me want to recoil at that thought, admittedly, I have to reapply my understanding. She has a fantastically scientific and precise account that took this from concept to reality for me. It's life-changing when incorporated into my core thinking.

Her accounting eased me in to what would otherwise have been way too woo-woo for me. Then came Dr. Wayne Dyer, who I can't even encapsulate, except to say that he is a loving, self propelling, kind, spiritual guru extraordinaire for anyone even moderately interested in self expansion and enlightenment. May he rest in peace!

The geneticist Bruce Lipton's groundbreaking, mind-blowing research taught me that we are not simply a product of our DNA blueprint. He showed that we are the product of our environment, including our thoughts, beliefs, and intentions. Thoughts truly become things, and literally changed the physical proteins in cell cultures that he studied. Thoughts changing matter, our bodies, and things found in reality? Totally outside my thinkin' box! In learning and playing with this information, the law of attraction and the reason it works became clear to me. Who or what we pray to for help is really just universally available energy that we have the power to tap into and affect, and the God idea became less scary. Life got way less creepy scary and more like a very badass, high yield "I actually care about this" science experiment with heart.

Joe Dispenza applies Lipton's concepts with a virtual layman's guidebook on how your brain really works for you *or* against you, and how to access your highest self, get rid of the old emotional junk, and recreate the being you want to be through self dissection, comprehension, and meditation. The quantum physical world is at large and manipulable.

Another significant influence in the NDE world, Eben Alexander, states "If you have a strong religious faith, you are most likely better off than someone who doesn't. But if you come, as I have, to see religion, spirituality, and science as partners in showing the universe as it truly is, I believe you can become even stronger."

Mind! Blown.

How are you supposed to control and enlighten these thoughts all the time, and even catch yourself doing it, what with 60-70 thousand thoughts and 80 million environmental inputs a day floating around, and only a tiny fraction of them original thoughts, that don't just pin-ballishly recur over and over in your record-skipping skull? It's right up there with Deepak Chopra's mind-bending lectures that indicate we are all just a figment of the imagination so to speak, but that's another chapter I'm not equipped to write.

I'm still working on these concepts and probably will be forever. I'm just glad to at least be starting the class at 40 years old, but still. If you're 20 reading this you will be killing it if you start now. Just sayin'.

Most other accounts of near death experiences that exist out there that say a similar same thing. Even characters who lived less than savory lives before their almost passing reported following a bright and beckoning light, and feeling an overwhelming and unchecked outpouring of love for them.

When I heard the stories of those authors listed above and numerous others, I could feel them strike a chord of truth that gives me goose bumps and makes the hair on my neck stand in salute. I knew it was true. Like the still small voice, or whatever is at work out there, it just rings real and right. The application and experimentation that comes with applying that knowledge reinforces and demystifies it considerably.

And life seems beautifully simple.

That is, if you can wrap your head around ideas that are against all things most of us have been taught about predictability and scientific method. I get confused and flustered with the complexity of thinking this stuff instead of just feeling through it sometimes. The roads to happy understanding and spiritual wealth don't have to be complicated. Carrie, my brilliant and soulful sister in law, always brings it back with the sage advice that "It all just comes back to kindness. We're all the same person, them and us and everyone in-between. Don't blow a fuse, just be as kind as you can no matter what they elicit. You can be laughing on the inside, just always let the kindness show through. The beautiful simplicity of the fully applied golden rule "Treat others as you would have them treat you" is enough for true happiness. The rest is an opportunity for growth and expansion. Not to be overdone, or steamy-eared mind blowing may occur, which hurts. I've done this many times.

CHAPTER 23

GRATITUDE

Ingrained in me in such a way that I don't usually recognize them, are many traits for which I thank the LDS church. Most of these things, save an unsettling expectation of the second coming of Christ, are traits that people find appealing and I continue to strive for. The church teaches the faithful to have a generally positive outlook; this still pervades many aspects of my life.

I am forever grateful for my parents, grandparents, and the other, truly good people who taught me over the years to aspire to kindness, "Christ-like behavior," and caring about another before myself. As a kid, I was taught via many church service projects and activities the value of hard work and having pride in the works I did, in pulling together and giving support to those in need in times of need or crisis. I was taught to have unconditional kindness and good intention, integrity, and to listen to my intuition (Holy Ghost, common sense yelling from your super-conscious mind, higher power, highest self; whatever you want to call it). I was told to always value honesty, even at a cost to you when it was told. In regard to doing good works, how to think with a type of universal consciousness bigger than myself, a kind of "hive mind." To have self-discipline and conscientious behavior as divulged in the Word of Wisdom. The Word of Wisdom is a law of health, or kind of life code Mormons live by that was decreed by God for the physical and spiritual benefit of His children. In 1833, in a revelation called Doctrine and Covenants, God revealed which foods are good for use and which substances should be avoided. He promised health, protection, knowledge, and wisdom to those who obey it. It encourages omissions of many things tempting for mankind like alcohol, caffeine such as coffee and tea, abuse of prescription and illegal drugs, and tobacco. It encourages to eat meat sparingly, and vegetables and fruits are to be used with prudence.

Another tenet of great value is that family comes first; in fact "families can be together forever" is one of the main hymns. Sundays are for church and family. You spend time, no matter how busy, with your parents and siblings. You grow through them, you find value in them, even if it doesn't come naturally. They are your people. You don't just grow up and pass the time with them, later figuring out how to avoid uncomfortable holiday gatherings with the strangers you call your family, years after you leave the nest. You have understanding—conflicts for sure, but you come to really know them, and there is the belief that we all chose each other in heaven to be with before we were born to this world. I do believe that families are not random. I think that the people in your family are right for you for some reason. Some pre-determined order in the universe or of your pre-life choosing that make them your people while you're here. I have sisters and brothers who are weird, amazing, and crazy soulmates. We have tested each other's patience and at times our ability to love, despite disassociation with each others' behaviors. I have learned volumes from each parent and sibling I have, and I hope I have given this back to them as well. I feel so blessed at the amazingness of my super-sized family, and when many people recoil in horror when I say I'm the oldest of eight with some step-brothers and sisters to boot, I have to laugh. It does sound crazy, and sometimes growing up in a household with anywhere from four to nine kids, it *was* crazy. It's nothing but good fortune, though, that brought some of the people I love and respect most in the world into my family. And they can't ditch me, because we're related! It's perfect. For me anyway.

As churches go, there are many good things about this one in particular that I don't want to overlook. I can understand why so many people are drawn to it. It's wholesome. A lot of good comes from that and should benefit people of all sexualities if they wish to get that kind of benefit from a church. We should all have the right to choose, or at least not be flat-out rejected and given the hand.

Chapter 24

Skippy Pants

Living now as I do an extra-ordinarily happy, married, and make-your-friends-hurl-a-little relationship, with no religious guilt and fear-free, I am out of the woods. (Except for the fear of walking through face-level spider webs, standing on anything higher than 12 feet from the ground, losing our jobs, bodily injury to friends or family, and of big trucks who drive over their line on the road). Nicole and I are slightly earthy-crunchy girls stuck in annoyingly aging bodies, whispering hippie-gone-modern mantras of good times, hard work, wishful lotto winning, self-help reading, hopeful, music loving, rowing and running, planet-saving, yoga-practicing, kid-adoring, traveling, reach-too-far-without-enough-time-in-the-day realizing, happily busy chiquitas. We wear our absence of high fashion and our love of gardening brown on our sleeves like proper Northwesterners, with the remnants of tomboyishness lurking ever so slightly. This is true until someone kicks a ball. Then Nicole might as well sprout a mullet, don some Carharts, and unfurl rainbow flags from both ears that flap in the wind as she compulsively races after it.

We're regular. In a perfectly ordinary but not ordinary way. We are just like most people, only it was harder for us to get here, and people still have to explain around the dinner table to their children that one of us isn't a boy, just a girl with short hair. And the birds and the bees, explaining that all families are different ... yadda, yadda. Eat your peas.

I had the occasion to personally ask Deepak Chopra to comment on alternate sexualities after he had given a talk on karma, universal consciousness, quantum physics, and other mind-blowing topics only Deepak can weave together. I was initially disappointed in his answer, thinking he would come up with some intricate and complicated geneto-karmic etiology of gay insightfulness. But he simply stated in his heavy accent "There have always been homosexual individuals and transsexuals in every society, in every culture through time. There is nothing good or bad about it. It just is."

BOOM. He sat there, with me staring expectantly at his T-shirt that broadcasted "SPIRITUAL GANGSTER", saying nothing more. He just sat there, smiling at me like he just told me where I lost my binky. He quoted someone I forgot, saying "Nothing human is foreign to me". I just kind of stood there, in the question que waiting for more dialogue; a diatribe of nature and nurture and akashic agreements and karmic need for self knowledge and stuff and stuff, then mind blowing-er stuff like Deepak tends to do.

But nothing else came.

I blinked audibly a few times, then sat down to think about his answer. Duh. This man knows that our reality is a product of what we make by our consciousness. He is one of the most advanced spiritual and scientific minds of our time, and this question was a near waste of his time. After marinating in his simplicity for a while, I realized how amazing this answer was, understanding that I'm still looking for reasons for difference when I should just be thankful for what I am. My differences made me who I am. A bird doesn't agonize over why he is blue and not red, why he pecks at trees, migrates in the cold, or wakes in the morning or at night. Why should we? We're not good or bad, not anomalies, mutations, or accidents. Suddenly I thought I had wasted my Deepak question, but now I had one more very valued "outside voice" that agreed with the inside voice I always had. Now we can all move on to bigger, and more uplifting topics! Let's move on together, and flounder as a community in the ideas of quantum thinking and the fact that we don't actually exist outside our thoughts. Gulp. Baby steps.

CHAPTER 25

A LIVING PROPHET

There are so very many good-hearted members of the church who are patiently poised to hear a more just ruling on this topic from the church. A vast majority of the LDS people I have spoken with agree, saying it needs (to quote a few): "updating," "further understanding," "softening," "re-evaluation," "evolving," "further contemplation and revelation," or "a more loving platform."

Many people say they don't really agree with "that part" of the church, but it doesn't bother them enough to leave the church. It just makes them "embarrassed" or "uncomfortable," because they don't want to associate with what they feel is a bigoted way of thinking. When asked, though, most say that they don't really know what to do about it. They are resigned that they can't change something as big and timeless as the church, and the thought of leaving creates a huge identity crisis. Admittedly the church stance shakes their faith, and they may wane in church dedication because of it. Many have stated that the church is "just slow" or run by members who are not really "modern in their thinking."

I can understand the conundrum. If you feel strongly enough about a religious difference to make a stand over it and not "follow along quietly", you face losing your culture, family approval, and relationships with friends. At least you think that's what you will be facing if you speak out, have had enough, and disavow that religious dictate. You have to really be convicted to go that far! And while those of us who have left the religion see it as being something that gets easier with time and calls up zero regret, those who face the consequences of leaving really suffer significant consequences, or perceived consequences to their lives.

After the LDS declaration in the fall of 2015 that same-sex couples are not only unwelcome, they are considered to be apostates, and then extended their judgement to not only those *living* the life that is true to them, but their *children* who are now restricted from baptism and other important church rites and membership as well. They denied the children of gay families membership! Many members felt it was time to break their ties with the church entirely after this ruling, and more than 1,500 people submitted their resignations the Saturday after the announcement, lining up for hours across the street from the church headquarters in order to make it formal. It's unknown how many have left since that day, but there were enough dissatisfied LGBT supporters and empathisers to cause a ripple of significance in church membership. The *New York Times* wrote, "The response of hundreds of members of the church was powerful. In recent days, Mormons have been leaving the church in droves, saying they no longer feel at home in an institution that so resolutely excludes a segment of the population that has become increasingly visible, legally protected, and socially accepted in America."

When I heard about this declaration, I couldn't believe how much it upset me. I had completely left the church and had many disagreements with the doctrine, but I *never* would have thought they would take action that was so severe and unfair. Even the *children* of gays, through no fault of their own, are ousted from the ranks of the church by association. And half of my family remained upstanding members of this church! I cried with shame, resurgent anger, and disgust. Then I cried because this religion still had the power to make me cry. Again. I cried thinking of all the heartbroken and ashamed LGBT kids who were not ready to leave the church and who would be further crushed inside by this rejection. The mean "Ken and Barbie" members with just one more reason to judge and reject another who are now all that more justified by a church's judgement.

Just being associated with this religion that was doing something so embarrassingly hateful was heartbreaking. I admitted, throwing understanding aside, that it was also made worse by knowing that so many of my loved ones would still remain followers. I was in shock. I expected painfully slow progress, not a bounding leap backward.

I contend that sitting back and waiting for the church to change its current stance is insufficient in a climate where kids and adults still kill themselves in shame for something they can't and shouldn't change. And the increase in gay suicide is indefinitely impacted. If a church still holds that the gay population is naturally faulty and we are sinful in our love, it's a stance that perpetuates mistreatment and misunderstanding, and members need to be able to see that for what it is. I'm not writing this to get Mormons to leave their religion if they love it and it perpetuates good. I urge you, if you disagree with this particular prophet's stance and current ruling to let your leaders know. Let it be known to those around you that you don't condone this way of treating others. In doing so you make it better. You don't have to quit the church, boycott with signs and leave your religion that nurtures and comforts your good.

Imagine a church that freely gave love and acceptance to anyone looking for spiritual progress. Who incorporated and married two people who loved each other without judgment of the gender of its members, with honor given to the desire for true commitment to one to another. Imagine following what your heart tells you is right, without a twinge of resistance based in religion about how you view and treat LGBT individuals. If you can imagine it, then it's closer to being true. John Lennon sang, "You may say I'm a dreamer, but I'm not the only one." We'll be in good company. If you are that Mormon, and you speak up about it, I guarantee you will not be standing alone, and the rejection you fear you will suffer will likely not be as severe as you fear. You may even effect real and needed change.

I recently attended an awards ceremony for the Greater Seattle Business Association, a chamber of commerce for lesbian, gay, bisexual, transgendered, and allied professionals. One of the scholarship recipients moved me to tears. She was the first and only scholarship recipient of the GSBA who *wasn't* gay, transgendered, or queer. She was a young heterosexual Hispanic woman who had made real sacrifices in her life for the rights of others, including leaving her beloved fiancé after noticing that he called a gay man a faggot. She had devoted a significant amount of time and energy to standing up for the rights of LGBT people. Just because! How many of us would go to those lengths when we *don't* have a loved one—son, daughter, close friend—who forces a choice into action. I have many family members who I know love me, but have made no move to action whatsoever. This woman not only wouldn't stand for hearing it, this shy girl then became a victor for our community. I'm amazed by this brand of empathetic and bold courage that few of us have without impetus.

We rely on our allies for forward progress, and I feel so very grateful for their growing numbers. I used to walk at night in my old neighborhood north of Seattle. Outside the city people tend to be less open, their views not as broad. I know this is gross stereotyping, but since I've lived this multiple times and it's true, I'll admit it. It's like trying to argue that lesbians on the whole don't flock to softball, black people don't excel in athletics, and gay men don't flock to fashion. Anyway, I was taking a neighborhood walk one night years ago holding hands with my partner Yvonne and we passed an older, very conservative and stern looking man and woman. We saw them coming and braced for discomfort, but kept holding hands, halting our conversation to a hushed side-mouthed mumble. As we went by, the man knocked my socks off my stereotyping, misguided feet by commenting, "Way to go, you girls. You're beautiful and you should be proud." My whole being overflows with thanks for people like that in the world. It's one thing to take up a cause that's your own, and a whole new level of human to take up causes you're personally "unaffected" by. Thanks to all of you, sincerely.

I'll wrap this up with the ally who most deeply touched my life. His name was Benjamin (I'm lying, I can't say his real name), and he was the college Psychological Counselor I worked with while struggling with my identity in my small art-school town. He was also a bishop in the church.

We had grown quite close. At least I had come to care deeply for him.

Benjamin had literally and figuratively held my hand through a full year of intensive Brandea analyzing in what was intended to be anti-gay therapy. I perched every Wednesday (and in emergencies, Saturdays too) in his cramped and paper-piled university office and memorized the floor. He was the first one I spilled the whole truth to (with a hat pulled down to my eyebrows and a hoodie on). If I ever thought I saw him on campus for the first few months, I would ditch the person I was with, wildly and ridiculously dodging in the other direction to avoid the humiliation of seeing him publically, as if by locking eyes I would be lofting my hideous secret into the atmosphere.

Benjamin's stuffy office smelled like turkey sandwiches and paper and safety. He turned out to be my biggest support, as I tried every method we could come up with to eradicate this anomaly of sexuality from my life. I had memorized his woven gray sweater, his kind and watery blue eyes, and the funny nose scrunch he would do when sniffling and fighting back tears. He would bring me my own handkerchief to use, as some weeks I would not even be able to engage with him. I would blurt out three sentences on confusion and frustration with God, loneliness and failure, then flop fish-like back on his slippery, brown leather chair to cover my eyes and moisten his few papery Kleenex, then my sleeve, then his ratty chair with my tears while he filled the time with what he had read or thought of for me to try that week. We struggled together until we both knew it not only would not work without causing real damage. He *did* halfheartedly offer shock therapy as a final resort, but when I asked him incredulously, "Are you serious?" he laughed and said no, but that he wanted to be complete so I knew he had offered every option available.

"Uh, doesn't that cause memory loss? I'm taking 21 credits this quarter. ... seriously? I'm a B student as it is." He rolled his eyes and said he didn't think that it would work anyway.

His parting words stuck in my heart and helped re-frame the way I thought of the world that loomed ahead of me.

He hugged me goodbye, and croaked, "I think you have done your due diligence. I am sure that God loves you. I don't understand why homosexuality exists, or its place in this church, but I will say without fear of being wrong, that I'm not worried for you in the afterlife. There is nothing wrong with you, and at this point, you should be true to who you are—a beautiful, smart young lady with so much to give and a great life ahead. I believe the right thing will happen in the end, even though we don't understand it now. Learn to love yourself, keep loving who you love, and just be."

I used to read and re-read that last journal entry when the going got tough in the years that followed. After being gay wasn't such a stinging wound in my life as it was then, I found myself applying that advice to everything else. Will I be a good enough parent? Am I smart enough to practice medicine? If I get on this Mexican zip line with my wife, will I die a horrible death?

Like the simple wisdom of "All I needed to know in life, I learned in Kindergarten", isn't it true that all you need to do is *trust* that you're just how you were supposed to be? Be the best you that you can be, and when choices are to be made, be true to you. Learn to love people for who they are, no matter what.

And just be.

AFTERWORD

It's hard to believe that hate crimes are still common in the United States and throughout the world. Gay youth suicide is rampant. Utah's suicide rate among those aged 15–24 is ninth highest in the United States; its overall suicide rate is the fifth highest in the country (Center for Disease Control, 2013). Suicide is the second leading cause of death for Utahns aged 10–17 (Utah Department of Health, 2012). In nine sites in the Midwest, Eastern U.S., and California, lesbian and gay high school attendees had a rate of attempted suicide that was approximately four times higher than for straight students (CDC, 2011). In 2014, almost 21 percent of hate crimes related to sexual orientation and gender identity.

It takes a-helluva-*lot* of bigotry for someone to physically hurt someone who is unlike him or herself. I could drum up more shocking and horrible statistics (many others have), but it's undisputed. And if you're like me you skim the belabored stats anyway. If nothing else, please understand that bigotry still hurts, and it still causes large numbers of tragically unnecessary deaths. There is dire need of a change.

About The Author

Brandea J. Kelley was born and raised in the Mormon heartland of the Utah valley. She now resides happily in Seattle Washington with her wife and two children, enjoying the close relationships of her extended family and friends.

She received her BS in Psychology from the University of Utah, and worked as a counselor for troubled youth prior to joining the Peace Corps in West Africa. She then continued her education at the University of Washington to become a Physician Assistant, and has practiced in Oncology, Urgent Care, and Surgery in her twelve years as a Advanced Practice Practitioner.

She is a Human Rights activist, art and music enthusiast, voracious reader, spiritual seeker, Qigong and meditation enthusiast, and lover of the outdoors. She is honored to serve on the board of two non-profit agencies: Global Impact (providing healthcare and service work to those in developing countries), and The Institute for Qigong and Integrative Medicine.

Please visit her website for more information.
www.mormongrowngay.com

Made in the USA
Middletown, DE
25 February 2020

85312218R00090